high tea

high tea

recipes with a sense of occasion

MURDOCH BOOKS

Contents

high tea

Little cakes

Orange poppy seed cupcakes

40 g (1½ oz/¼ cup) poppy seeds,
   plus extra to sprinkle
125 ml (4 fl oz/½ cup) warm milk
150 g (5½ oz) unsalted butter, softened
3 teaspoons finely grated orange zest
170 g (6 oz/¾ cup) caster (superfine) sugar
2 eggs
185 g (6½ oz/1½ cups) self-raising flour, sifted

Citrus icing (frosting)
250 g (9 oz) unsalted butter, softened
375 g (13 oz/3 cups) icing (confectioners') sugar,
   sifted
3 teaspoons finely grated orange zest

makes
15

Preheat the oven to 180°C (350°F/Gas 4).
Line 15 standard muffin holes with paper cases.

Combine the poppy seeds and milk in a bowl and set
aside for at least 15 minutes.

Place the butter, orange zest, caster sugar, eggs and
flour in a large bowl. Add the poppy seed mixture
and beat with electric beaters on low speed until
combined. Increase to a medium speed and beat for
3 minutes, or until the mixture is thick and pale.

Divide the mixture evenly among the cases. Bake for
15 minutes, or until a skewer comes out clean when
inserted in the centre of a cake. Transfer to a wire
rack to cool.

To make the citrus icing, place the butter, icing sugar
and zest in a large bowl and beat with electric
beaters until light and fluffy. Spread the icing over
the cakes and sprinkle with the extra poppy seeds.

Butterfly cupcakes

Preheat the oven to 180°C (350°F/Gas 4). Line 12 standard muffin holes with paper cases.

Beat butter, sugar, flour, milk and eggs with electric beaters on low speed until combined. Increase to medium speed and beat until the mixture is smooth and pale.

Divide the mixture evenly among the cases and bake for 15–20 minutes, or until a skewer comes out clean when inserted in the centre of a cake. Transfer to a wire rack to cool.

Cut a shallow round from the centre of each cake using the point of a sharp knife, then cut the round in half. Spoon 2 teaspoons of cream into the cavity of each cake, then top with 1 teaspoon of jam. Position the two halves of the cake round in the jam to make butterfly wings. Sprinkle with sifted icing sugar.

120 g (4¼ oz) unsalted butter, softened
145 g (5 oz/⅔ cup) caster (superfine) sugar
185 g (6½ oz/1½ cups) self-raising flour
125 ml (4 fl oz/½ cup) milk
2 eggs
125 ml (4 fl oz/½ cup) thick (double/heavy) cream
80 g (1½ oz/¼ cup) strawberry jam
icing (confectioners') sugar, to sprinkle

makes
12

Neenish cupcakes

250 g (9 oz) unsalted butter

230 g (8½ oz/1 cup) caster (superfine) sugar

1 teaspoon natural vanilla extract

4 eggs

185 g (6½ oz/1½ cups) self-raising flour, sifted

60 g (2¼ oz/½ cup) plain (all-purpose) flour, sifted

185 ml (6 fl oz/¾ cup) milk

30 g (1 oz/¼ cup) unsweetened cocoa powder, sifted

Icing (frosting)

185 g (6½ oz/1½ cups) icing (confectioners') sugar, sifted

10 g (¼ oz) unsalted butter

Chocolate topping

200 g (7 oz) dark chocolate, roughly chopped

makes
16

Preheat the oven to 180°C (350°F/Gas 4). Line 16 standard muffin holes with paper cases.

Beat butter, sugar and vanilla together with electric beaters until light and creamy. Add the eggs, one at a time, beating well after each addition. Fold in the flours alternately with the milk. Divide the mixture in half and stir cocoa through one half of the mixture until well combined. Divide the chocolate mixture evenly into half of the cases. Then divide the plain mixture into the other half, so that each case is filled with half chocolate and half plain mixtures. Bake for 18–20 minutes, or until a skewer comes out clean when inserted in the centre of a cake. Transfer to a wire rack to cool.

To make white icing, place the icing sugar and butter in a small heatproof bowl. Stir in enough warm water to form a smooth paste. Sit the bowl over a small saucepan of simmering water and stir until smooth and glossy. Remove from the heat. Spread the icing over the white side of each cake.

To make the chocolate topping, place the chocolate in a small bowl over a saucepan of simmering water, and stir occasionally until the chocolate has melted. Spread the chocolate over the other half of the cakes.

Apricot, sour cream and coconut cupcakes

220 g (7¾ oz/1¾ cups) self-raising flour

45 g (1⅔ oz/½ cup) desiccated coconut

125 g (4½ oz) unsalted butter

230 g (8½ oz/1 cup) caster (superfine) sugar

2 eggs, lightly beaten

250 ml (9 fl oz/1 cup) apricot nectar

125 g (4½ oz/½ cup) sour cream

825 g (1 lb 13 oz) tinned apricot halves in juice,
   drained (you need 20 apricot halves)

80 g (2¾ oz/¼ cup) apricot jam

makes
20

Preheat the oven to 180°C (350°F/Gas 4).
Line 20 standard muffin holes with paper cases.

Sift the flour into a large mixing bowl, then add the coconut and make a well in the centre. Melt the butter and sugar in a small saucepan over low heat, stirring until the sugar has dissolved. Remove from the heat. Whisk the combined egg and apricot nectar into the sour cream. Add both the butter and the egg mixtures to the well in the dry ingredients and stir with a wooden spoon until combined.

Divide the mixture evenly among the cases and place an apricot half, cut side up, on the top of each cake. Bake for 18–20 minutes, or until a skewer comes out clean when inserted in the centre of a cake. Transfer to a wire rack to cool.

Heat the jam in a small saucepan over a gentle heat until melted. Brush a little jam over each cake.

Apple and raisin cupcakes

Preheat the oven to 180°C (350°F/Gas 4). Line 12 standard muffin holes with paper cases.

Sift the flour into a large bowl and make a well in the centre. Melt the butter and sugar in a small saucepan over a low heat, stirring until the sugar has dissolved. Remove from the heat. Combine the raisins and apple purée with the butter mixture. Pour into the well in the flour, along with the egg. Stir with a wooden spoon until combined.

Divide the mixture evenly among the cases. Bake for 15 minutes, or until a skewer comes out clean when inserted in the centre of a cake. Transfer to a wire rack to cool completely.

To make yoghurt topping, combine the yoghurt and sugar. Spread 1 tablespoon of topping over each cake.

185 g (6½ oz/1½ cups) self-raising flour

150 g (5½ oz) unsalted butter, chopped

140 g (5 oz/¾ cup) soft brown sugar

125 g (4½ oz/1 cup) raisins, plus extra
   to garnish

120 g (4¼ oz) apple purée

3 eggs, lightly beaten

Yoghurt topping

250 g (9 oz/1 cup) plain yoghurt

1 tablespoon soft brown sugar

makes
12

Apple pecan cupcakes

310 g (11 oz/2½ cups) self-raising flour

1½ teaspoons ground cinnamon

165 g (5¾ oz/¾ cup) caster (superfine) sugar

2 granny smith apples (about 340 g/11¾ oz),
   peeled, cored and coarsely grated

50 g (1¾ oz/½ cup) pecans, chopped

2 eggs, lightly beaten

125 ml (4 fl oz/½ cup) milk

15 g (½ oz) unsalted butter, melted

thick (double/heavy) cream or yoghurt, to serve
   (optional)

makes
16

Preheat the oven to 180°C (350°F/Gas 4).
Line 16 standard muffin holes with paper cases.

Combine flour, cinnamon, sugar, apple and pecans in
a bowl. Add the egg, milk and melted butter, stirring
until the mixture is just combined and smooth.

Divide the mixture evenly among the cases. Bake for
18–20 minutes, or until a skewer comes out clean
when inserted in the centre of a cake. Transfer to a
wire rack to cool.

If desired, sprinkle with icing sugar and serve with
thick cream or yoghurt.

Little plum cakes with coffee caramel

150 g (5½ oz) unsalted butter, softened

140 g (5 oz/¾ cup) soft brown sugar

2 eggs

165 g (5¾ oz/1⅓ cups) plain (all-purpose) flour

1½ teaspoons baking powder

¼ teaspoon freshly grated nutmeg

125 g (4½ oz/½ cup) plain yoghurt

3 firm ripe plums or small peaches, halved and
   thinly sliced

Coffee caramel

170 g (6 oz/¾ cup) caster (superfine) sugar

80 ml (2½ fl oz/⅓ cup) freshly made hot espresso
   coffee

makes
10

To make the coffee caramel, place the sugar and 80 ml (2½ fl oz/⅓ cup) water in a small heavy-based saucepan over medium heat and stir to dissolve the sugar. Bring to the boil, without stirring, and cook the syrup until golden brown. Immediately remove from the heat, carefully pour in the coffee—beware, the caramel will splutter and spit—and stir to combine. Transfer to a heatproof jug and set aside.

Preheat the oven to 180°C (350°F/Gas 4). Grease ten 125 ml (4 fl oz/½ cup) friand tins.

Using electric beaters, cream the butter and sugar in a large bowl until pale and fluffy. Add the eggs, one at a time, beating well after each addition. Sift in the flour, baking powder and nutmeg, then add the yoghurt and mix well. Spoon the batter into the prepared tins and arrange the fruit slices on top. Bake for 20–25 minutes, or until a skewer inserted in the centre of a cake comes out clean. Turn out onto a wire rack to cool.

Serve the cakes warm with a drizzle of coffee caramel.

Chocolate beetroot cakes

canola oil spray, to grease

125 g (4½ oz/1 cup) plain (all-purpose) flour

40 g (1½ oz/⅓ cup) unsweetened cocoa powder

1½ teaspoons bicarbonate of soda (baking soda)

½ teaspoon baking powder

1 teaspoon mixed (pumpkin pie) spice (optional)

230 g (8 oz/1 cup) soft brown sugar

75 g (2¾ oz/¾ cup) walnut halves, chopped

170 ml (5½ fl oz/⅔ cup) canola or vegetable oil

2 eggs, at room temperature

225 g (8 oz/1½ cups) coarsely grated beetroot

unsweetened cocoa powder, sifted, for dusting

thick (double/heavy) cream or vanilla ice cream
   (optional)

makes
12

Preheat the oven to 180°C (350°F/Gas 4). Spray twelve 125 ml (4 fl oz/½ cup) fluted ring tins with the oil and place on a baking tray.

Sift the flour, cocoa, bicarbonate of soda, baking powder and mixed spice, if using, into a large bowl. Stir in sugar and walnuts. Make a well in the centre.

Whisk the oil and eggs in a medium-sized bowl until well combined, then stir in the beetroot. Fold into the flour mixture using a large metal spoon. Spoon into the prepared tins and smooth the surfaces with the back of a spoon. Bake for 20 minutes, or until a skewer inserted in the centre of a cake comes out clean. Allow to stand in the tins for 5 minutes, then turn out onto a wire rack to cool completely.

Dust with cocoa and serve with the cream or ice cream, if desired.

These cakes will keep, stored in an airtight container, for up to 3 days.

Beehive cupcakes

200 g (7 oz) unsalted butter, softened

185 g (6½ oz/1 cup) soft brown sugar

3 eggs

115 g (4 oz/⅓ cup) honey, warmed

280 g (10 oz/2¼ cups) self-raising flour, sifted

Marshmallow icing (frosting)

3 egg whites

330 g (11¾ oz/1½ cups) sugar

2 teaspoons light corn syrup

pinch of cream of tartar

1 teaspoon natural vanilla extract

yellow food colouring

15 toothpicks

15 chocolate-foil wrapped bumble bees with wings

makes
15

Preheat the oven 180°C (350°F/Gas 4). Line 15 standard muffin holes with paper cases.

Beat the butter and sugar with electric beaters until light and creamy. Add eggs, one at a time, beating well after each addition. Fold in the honey and flour until combined. Divide the mixture evenly among the cases. Bake for 18–20 minutes, or until a skewer comes out clean when inserted in the centre of a cake. Transfer to a wire rack to cool.

To make the marshmallow icing, combine the egg whites, sugar, corn syrup, cream of tartar and 100 ml (3½ fl oz) of water in a heatproof bowl. Sit the bowl over a saucepan of simmering water, making sure the bowl doesn't touch the water. Using electric beaters, beat for 5 minutes, or until the mixture is light and fluffy. Remove from the heat. Add the vanilla and beat with electric beaters for 4–5 minutes, or until stiff peaks form. Add the colouring, drop by drop, and beat until just combined.

Spoon the icing into a piping bag fitted with a 1 cm (½ inch) round nozzle, and pipe the icing in circles around the cake to resemble a beehive. Push the pointy end of a toothpick into the base of each bumble bee and insert it in each cake.

Prune and ricotta cupcakes

Preheat the oven to 180°C (350°F/Gas 4). Line 18 mini muffin holes with paper cases.

Combine prunes and Marsala in a small saucepan. Bring to the boil, then reduce the heat and simmer for 30 seconds, or until the Marsala is absorbed. Allow to cool.

Beat the ricotta and sugar with electric beaters for 2 minutes, or until light and creamy. Gradually add eggs, one at a time, beating well after each addition. Add the cream and beat for 2 minutes. Using a metal spoon, fold in the sifted cornflour and flour, the prune mixture and the chocolate.

Divide the mixture evenly among the cases. Bake for 15–18 minutes, or until firm to the touch and lightly golden. Transfer to a wire rack to cool. Sprinkle with icing sugar just before serving.

75 g (2⅔ oz/⅓ cup) pitted prunes, chopped

1 tablespoon Marsala

250 g (9 oz) ricotta

115 g (4 oz/½ cup) caster (superfine) sugar

2 eggs

60 ml (2 fl oz/¼ cup) whipping cream

30 g (1 oz/¼ cup) cornflour (cornstarch), sifted

2 tablespoons self-raising flour, sifted

30 g (1 oz/¼ cup) grated dark chocolate

makes
18

Individual blueberry cheesecakes

Cheese mixture

115 g (4 oz/½ cup) caster (superfine) sugar

85 g (3 oz/⅓ cup) cream cheese

Blueberry sauce

250 g (9 oz/1⅔ cups) blueberries

1 tablespoon crème de cassis

165 g (5¾ oz/1⅓ cups) plain (all-purpose) flour

1 tablespoon baking powder

20 g (¾ oz) unsalted butter, melted

1 teaspoon finely grated orange zest

1 egg

125 ml (4 fl oz/½ cup) milk

18 blueberries, extra, for filling

icing (confectioners') sugar, to sprinkle

makes
6

Preheat the oven to 180°C (350°F/Gas 4). Lightly grease 6 standard muffin holes with butter or oil.

To make the cheese mixture, put half the sugar in a bowl with the cream cheese and combine well.

To make the blueberry sauce, put the blueberries in a blender or food processor with the liqueur and remaining sugar, and blend until smooth. Strain the mixture through a fine sieve to remove any blueberry seeds. Set the cheese mixture and sauce aside.

Sift the flour and baking powder together in a large bowl and stir in the butter, orange zest and ½ teaspoon of salt. In a separate bowl, beat the egg and milk together, then add to the dry ingredients and mix well until combined.

Divide half the mixture evenly among the holes. Add three of the extra blueberries and 1 teaspoon of cheese mixture in each hole, then top with the remaining batter mixture. Bake for 15 minutes, or until cooked and golden. Transfer to a wire rack to cool slightly.

To serve, put each cheesecake on a plate, drizzle with blueberry sauce and sprinkle with icing sugar.

Mini pear and walnut cupcakes

150 g (5½ oz) unsalted butter, softened

140 g (5 oz/¾ cup) soft brown sugar

2 eggs

155 g (5½ oz/1¼ cups) self-raising flour, sifted

125 ml (4 fl oz/½ cup) milk

135 g (3½ oz/½ cup) tinned pears, well drained
  and chopped

40 g (1½ oz/⅓ cup) chopped walnuts

Maple cream icing (frosting)

90 g (3¼ oz) cream cheese, softened

60 ml (2 fl oz/¼ cup) maple syrup

185 g (6½ oz/1½ cups) icing (confectioners') sugar,
  sifted

60 g (2¼ oz/½ cup) chopped walnuts, to decorate

makes
36

Preheat the oven to 180°C (350°F/Gas 4).
Line 36 mini muffin holes with paper cases.

Beat the butter and sugar together with electric beaters until light and creamy. Add the eggs, one at a time, beating well after each addition. Fold in the flour alternately with the milk. Fold in the pears and the walnuts. Divide the mixture evenly among the cases. Bake for 12–15 minutes, or until a skewer comes out clean when inserted into the centre of a cake. Transfer onto a wire rack to cool.

To make the maple cream icing, beat the cream cheese and maple syrup with electric beaters until combined. Gradually beat in the icing sugar until combined. Spread the icing over each cake and decorate with chopped walnuts.

Apple and coffee tea cakes

185 g (6½ oz/1½ cups) plain (all-purpose) flour

1 teaspoon ground cinnamon

¼ teaspoon ground allspice

¾ teaspoon baking powder

¾ teaspoon bicarbonate of soda (baking soda)

125 ml (4 fl oz/½ cup) buttermilk

80 ml (2½ fl oz/⅓ cup) freshly made espresso
coffee, cooled

185 g (6½ oz/¾ cup) unsalted butter, softened

140 g (5 oz/¾ cup) soft brown sugar

115 g (4 oz/½ cup) caster (superfine) sugar

2 teaspoons finely grated lemon zest

3 eggs

1 granny smith or golden delicious apple, peeled,
cored and thinly sliced

Streusel topping

¼ teaspoon ground allspice

45 g (1¾ oz/¼ cup) soft brown sugar

30 g (1 oz/¼ cup) plain (all-purpose) flour

60 g (2¼ oz/½ cup) chopped pecans

45 g (1¾ oz) unsalted butter, chilled and cut
into cubes

makes
8

Preheat the oven to 180°C (350°F/Gas 4). Grease eight 6 x 8 cm (2½ x 3¼ inch) cake tins and line the base and sides of each tin with baking paper.

To make the streusel topping, place the allspice, sugar, flour and pecans in a small bowl and rub in the butter with your fingertips until the mixture resembles coarse breadcrumbs. Set aside.

Sift flour, spices, baking powder and bicarbonate of soda into a bowl and set aside. Combine the buttermilk and coffee in a separate bowl.

Using electric beaters, cream the butter and sugars in a third bowl until pale and fluffy, then stir in the zest. Add the eggs, one at a time, beating well after each addition. Fold in the flour mixture, alternately with the buttermilk mixture, stirring until just combined and smooth. Stir in the apple slices.

Spoon batter into the prepared tins and smooth the surface with the back of a spoon. Bake cakes for 10 minutes, then remove from the oven and sprinkle streusel mixture over the top. Return to the oven for a further 15 minutes or until golden brown and a skewer inserted in the centre of a cake comes out clean. Cool for 10 minutes in the tins, then transfer to wire racks to cool completely.

Serve warm or at room temperature. (For image, see page 26.)

NOTE Twelve smaller cakes can be made using 4 x 8 cm (1½ x 3¼ inch) tins. Bake for 20 minutes.

Sour cream and coffee walnut cakes

60 g (2¼ oz/⅓ cup) soft brown sugar

75 g (2¾ oz/¾ cup) walnut halves

1 teaspoon finely ground espresso coffee beans

1 teaspoon ground cinnamon

115 g (4 oz) unsalted butter, softened

115 g (4 oz/½ cup) caster (superfine) sugar

2 eggs

185 g (6½ oz/1½ cups) plain (all-purpose) flour

¾ teaspoon baking powder

½ teaspoon bicarbonate of soda (baking soda)

225 g (8 oz) sour cream

10 walnut halves, to decorate

Icing (frosting)

155 g (5½ oz/1¼ cups) icing (confectioners')
    sugar, sifted

2–3 teaspoons freshly made strong
    espresso coffee

makes
10

Preheat the oven to 180°C (350°F/Gas 4). Grease 10 friand tins and line the bases with baking paper.

Place the brown sugar, walnuts, ground coffee and cinnamon in the bowl of a food processor and pulse until the mixture resembles coarse breadcrumbs. Add 40 g (1½ oz) of butter and process until well combined. Set aside.

Cream remaining butter and the caster sugar in a bowl using electric beaters until pale and fluffy. Add the eggs, one at a time, beating well after each addition. Sift flour, baking powder and bicarbonate of soda into a separate bowl. Stir one-third of the flour mixture, then one-third of the sour cream, into the egg mixture, and continue alternating until all the flour mixture and the sour cream is incorporated and the mixture well combined.

Spoon half the batter into the prepared tins and spread across the base. Sprinkle the reserved walnut mixture over the batter, then spoon on the remaining batter to cover evenly. Bake for 20–25 minutes, or until lightly golden and a skewer inserted in the centre of a cake comes out clean. Set aside to cool slightly in the tins, then turn out onto a wire rack to cool completely.

To make the icing, place the sugar in a bowl and stir in enough coffee, adding a little water if necessary, to make a smooth, spreadable consistency.

Spread the icing over the cakes and place a walnut half on top. Allow icing to cool before serving. (For image, see page 27.)

Orange and lemon syrup cupcakes

125 g (4½ oz) unsalted butter,
   chilled and chopped
230 g (8½ oz/1 cup) caster (superfine) sugar
2 teaspoons finely grated lemon zest
2 teaspoons finely grated orange zest
3 eggs
125 ml (4 fl oz/½ cup) milk
185 g (6½ oz/1½ cups) self-raising flour, sifted

Lemon syrup
230 g (8½ oz/1 cup) caster (superfine) sugar
zest of 1 lemon, thinly sliced
zest of 1 orange, thinly sliced

makes
36

Preheat the oven to 180°C (350°F/Gas 4).
Line 36 mini muffin holes with paper cases.

Place butter, sugar and lemon and orange zests in a saucepan and stir over low heat until the sugar has dissolved. Transfer to a large bowl. Add the eggs, milk and flour and beat with electric beaters until the ingredients are just combined.

Divide the mixture evenly among the cases. Bake for 15 minutes, or until a skewer comes out clean when inserted in the centre of a cake. Transfer onto a wire rack to cool.

To make the lemon syrup, place 200 ml (7 fl oz) of water and the sugar in a saucepan over a low heat, stirring until the sugar has dissolved. Add the lemon and orange zests, bring to the boil and simmer for 10 minutes, stirring occasionally, or until lightly golden and syrupy.

Strain the syrup, reserving the zest. Decorate each cake with some strips of zest and pour over a little of the syrup.

Hazelnut cream sponge cakes

Preheat the oven to 180°C (350°F/Gas 4). Grease a shallow 20 cm (8 inch) square cake tin and line the base with baking paper.

Beat the egg whites in a clean bowl with electric beaters until soft peaks form. Gradually add the sugar, beating until thick and glossy. Beat the egg yolks into the mixture, one at a time.

Sift the flour over the mixture, add the ground hazelnuts and fold in with a metal spoon. Melt the butter with 2 tablespoons of boiling water in a small bowl, then fold into the sponge mixture. Pour the mixture into the tin and bake for 25 minutes, or until a skewer comes out clean when inserted in the centre of the cake. Leave in the tin for 5 minutes before turning out onto a wire rack to cool. Cut the sponge in half horizontally through the centre.

To make the hazelnut icing, beat the chocolate hazelnut spread and butter with electric beaters until very creamy. Beat in the icing sugar, then gradually add 3 teaspoons of boiling water. Beat until smooth. Spread the icing over the base of the sponge, then replace the top layer. Refrigerate until the filling is firm, then cut into squares and place in paper cases.

4 eggs, separated

115 g (4 oz/½ cup) caster (superfine) sugar

60 g (2¼ oz/½ cup) self-raising flour

75 g (3 oz/⅔ cup) ground hazelnuts

20 g (¾ oz) unsalted butter

Hazelnut icing (frosting)

170 g (6 oz/½ cup) chocolate hazelnut spread

130 g (4¾ oz) unsalted butter, softened

60 g (2¼ oz/½ cup) icing (confectioners') sugar, sifted

makes
16

Marble patty cakes

185 g (6½ oz) unsalted butter, softened

170 g (6 oz/¾ cup) caster (superfine) sugar

1 teaspoon natural vanilla extract

3 eggs

125 g (4½ oz/1 cup) self-raising flour

30 g (1 oz/¼ cup) plain (all-purpose) flour

125 ml (4 fl oz/½ cup) milk

pink food colouring

2 tablespoons unsweetened cocoa powder, sifted

Marble icing (frosting)

280 g (10 oz/2¼ cups) icing (confectioners') sugar, sifted

100 g (3½ oz) unsalted butter, softened

pink food colouring

makes
10

Preheat the oven to 180°C (350°F/Gas 4). Line 10 standard muffin holes with paper cases.

Beat the butter, sugar and vanilla together with electric beaters until light and creamy. Add the eggs, one at a time, beating well after each addition. Sift the flours together and fold in alternately with milk.

Divide the mixture into three equal portions. Add a few drops of pink food colouring to one portion and mix to combine. Add the cocoa to another portion and mix to combine. Divide the three colours evenly into each case and gently swirl the mixture with a skewer. Bake for 15 minutes, or until a skewer comes out clean when inserted in the centre of a cake. Transfer onto a wire rack to cool.

To make the marble icing, mix the icing sugar, butter and sufficient hot water to make a spreadable icing. Spread the icing over each cake. Dip a skewer in pink food colouring and swirl it through the icing to create a marbled effect.

Madeira cupcakes

180 g (6½ oz) unsalted butter, softened

170 g (6 oz/¾ cup) caster (superfine) sugar

3 eggs

165 g (5¾ oz/1⅓ cups) plain (all-purpose) flour

2 teaspoons baking powder

1 teaspoon finely grated orange zest

1 tablespoon orange juice

Orange icing (frosting)

250 g (9 oz/2 cups) icing (confectioners')
   sugar, sifted

125 g (4½ oz) unsalted butter, softened

1 tablespoon orange juice

makes
12

Preheat the oven to 180°C (350°/Gas 4).
Line 12 standard muffin holes with paper cases.

Beat the butter and sugar in a bowl, with electric beaters until pale and light. Add the eggs, one at a time, beating well after each addition. Sift the flour and baking powder together. Fold the flour, orange zest and juice into the butter mixture until combined.

Divide the mixture evenly among the cases. Bake for 12–15 minutes, or until a skewer comes out clean when inserted in the centre of a cake. Transfer onto a wire rack to cool completely.

To make the orance icing, place the icing sugar, butter and juice in a large bowl and beat with electric beaters until smooth and well combined. Decorate each cake with icing and sprinkle with icing sugar.

Rich dark chocolate cupcakes

150 g (5½ oz) unsalted butter, chopped

200 g (7 oz) dark chocolate chips

185 g (6½ oz/1½ cups) self-raising flour

30 g (1 oz/¼ cup) unsweetened cocoa powder

285 g (10 oz/1¼ cups) caster (superfine) sugar

2 eggs, lightly beaten

chocolate curls, to decorate

Chocolate topping

250 g (9 oz) dark chocolate, chopped

40 g (1½ oz) unsalted butter

makes
18

Preheat the oven to 160°C (315°F/Gas 2–3). Line 18 standard muffin holes with paper cases.

Place the butter and chocolate chips in a small heatproof bowl. Sit the bowl over a saucepan of simmering water, making sure the bowl doesn't touch the water. Stir the chocolate constantly until it is melted.

Sift the flour and cocoa into a large bowl. Combine the melted butter and chocolate mixture, sugar and egg, then add 185 ml (6 fl oz/¾ cup) of water and mix well. Add to the dry ingredients and stir until well combined. Divide the mixture evenly among the cases. Bake for 20–25 minutes, or until a skewer comes out clean when inserted in the centre of a cake. Transfer onto a wire rack to cool.

To make the chocolate topping, place the chocolate and butter in a small heatproof bowl and sit it over a saucepan of simmering water, making sure the base of the bowl doesn't touch the water. Stir chocolate constantly until it melts. Decorate each cake with the topping and chocolate curls.

Pecan and orange cupcakes

125 g (4½ oz) unsalted butter, softened

170 g (6 oz/¾ cup) caster (superfine) sugar

2 eggs

100 g (3½ oz/¾ cup) ground pecans

3 teaspoons finely grated orange zest

185 g (6½ oz/1½ cups) self-raising flour, sifted

125 ml (4 fl oz/½ cup) milk

Cinnamon icing (frosting)

15 g (½ oz) unsalted butter, softened

¾ teaspoon ground cinnamon

185 g (6½ oz/1½ cups) icing (confectioners') sugar,
   sifted

makes
16 standard
24 mini

Preheat the oven to 180°C (350°F/Gas 4). Line 16 standard (or 24 mini) muffin holes with paper cases.

Beat butter and sugar with electric beaters until pale and creamy. Gradually add the eggs, one at a time, beating well after each addition. Add the ground pecans and orange zest, then use a metal spoon to gently fold in the flour alternately with the milk.

Divide the mixture evenly among the cases. Bake for 50–60 minutes (40 minutes for minis), or until a skewer comes out clean when inserted in the centre of a cake. Leave in the tin for 10 minutes, then transfer to a wire rack to cool.

To make the icing, combine the butter, icing sugar and cinnamon in a small bowl with 1½ tablespoons of hot water. Sit the bowl over a saucepan of simmering water, making sure the bowl doesn't touch the water, and stir until smooth and glossy. Remove from the heat. Decorate each cake with icing.

Chocolate cupcakes with ice cream

185 g (6 oz) unsalted butter

330 g (11¾ oz) caster (superfine) sugar

2½ teaspoons natural vanilla extract

3 eggs

5 g (2½ oz/⅔ cup) self-raising flour, sifted

220 g (7¾ oz/1¾ cups) plain (all-purpose)
  flour, sifted

1½ teaspoons bicarbonate of soda
  (baking soda), sifted

90 g (3 oz/¾ cup) unsweetened cocoa powder

250 ml (9 fl oz/1 cup) buttermilk

small scoops vanilla ice cream

makes
10

Preheat oven to 180°C (350°F/Gas 4). Lightly grease 10 standard muffin holes with melted butter or oil.

Beat the butter and sugar with electric beaters until light and creamy. Beat in the vanilla. Add the eggs, one at a time, beating well after each addition.

Fold in the combined flours, bicarbonate of soda and cocoa powder with a metal spoon, alternating with the buttermilk. Stir until just smooth.

Divide the mixture evenly among the holes. Bake for 25 minutes, or until a skewer comes out clean when inserted in the centre of a cake. Leave the cakes to cool in the tins for 5 minutes, then transfer onto a wire rack to cool completely.

With a sharp knife, cut out the centre of each cake, leaving a 1 cm (½ inch) border around the top. Keep the tops of the cakes to one side. Fill the centre of each cake with a small scoop of ice cream, then put the cake top on top.

Frangipani cupcakes

185 g (6½ oz) unsalted butter, softened

170 g (6 oz/¾ cup) caster (superfine) sugar

1 teaspoon vanilla extract

3 eggs

125 g (4½ oz/1 cup) self-raising flour

60 g (2¼ oz/½ cup) plain (all-purpose) flour

125 ml (4 fl oz/½ cup) milk

45 g (1½ oz/1 cup) pink and white mallow bakes

8 white marshmallows, quartered

8 pink marshmallows, quartered

yellow decorating gel

Icing (frosting)

375 g (13 oz/3 cups) icing (confectioners') sugar,
    sifted

2 egg whites

pink food colouring

makes
16

Preheat the oven to 180°C (350°F/Gas 4).
Line 16 standard muffin holes with large cases.

Beat the butter, sugar and vanilla together with electric beaters until light and creamy. Add the eggs, one at a time, beating well after each addition. Sift the flours together and fold in alternately with the milk. Stir through the mallow bakes until combined.

Divide the mixture evenly among the cases. Bake for 15 minutes, or until a skewer comes out clean when inserted in the centre of a cake. Transfer to a wire rack to cool.

To make the icing, beat the icing sugar and egg whites together for 5 minutes until white and fluffy. Divide the icing evenly into two separate bowls. Colour one with food colouring to make a pale pink.

Decorate half the cakes with pink icing and arrange white marshmallow quarters to resemble a flower on each cake. Repeat with the white icing and pink marshmallows for the remaining cakes. Squeeze a dollop of the yellow gel in the centre of all the marshmallow petals.

Rhubarb yoghurt cupcakes

150 g (5½ oz/1½ cups) finely sliced fresh
   rhubarb, plus 24 extra pieces to garnish
310 g (11 oz/2½ cups) self-raising flour, sifted
230 g (8½ oz/1 cup) caster (superfine) sugar
1 teaspoon natural vanilla extract
2 eggs, lightly beaten
125 g (4½ oz/½ cup) plain yoghurt
1 tablespoon rosewater
125 g (4½ oz) unsalted butter, melted

makes
24

Preheat the oven to 180°C (350°F/Gas 4).
Line 24 standard muffin holes with paper cases.

Combine the rhubarb, flour and sugar in a bowl.
Add the vanilla, egg, yoghurt, rosewater and the
melted butter, stirring with a wooden spoon until
the mixture is just combined.

Divide the mixture evenly among the cases, then top
with a piece of rhubarb. Bake for 15 minutes, or until
a skewer comes out clean when inserted in the centre
of a cake. Transfer to a wire rack to cool.

Honey, banana and macadamia cupcakes

100 g (3½ oz) unsalted butter, chopped

350 g (12 oz/1 cup) honey, plus extra to drizzle

250 g (9 oz/2 cups) self-raising flour

1 teaspoon mixed spice

150 g (5½ oz/1½ cups) coarsely grated carrot

1 ripe banana, mashed

70 g (2½ oz/½ cup) chopped macadamia nuts, plus
   extra, to sprinkle

2 eggs, lightly beaten

makes
32

Preheat the oven to 180°C (350°F/Gas 4).
Line 32 mini muffin holes with paper cases.

Melt the butter and honey in a small saucepan,
stirring until combined. Allow to cool.

Sift the flour and mixed spice into a large bowl. Add
the carrot, banana, macadamias, eggs and honey
mixture, stirring until the mixture is just combined
and smooth.

Divide the mixture evenly among the cases, and
sprinkle the tops liberally with extra chopped
macadamias. Bake for 8 minutes, or until a skewer
comes out clean when inserted in the centre of a
cake. Transfer to a wire rack to cool.

Drizzle a little honey over the cakes before serving.

Coffee swirl cheesecakes

150 g (5½ oz) caster (superfine) sugar

500 g (1 lb 2 oz/2 cups) cream cheese, softened

3 eggs

2 egg yolks

140 g (5 oz) sour cream

60 ml (2 fl oz/¼ cup) freshly made strong espresso
   coffee, cooled

2 tablespoons plain (all-purpose) flour

75 g (2¾ oz) dark chocolate, melted and cooled

2 tablespoons Kahlua or other coffee-flavoured
   liqueur

Base

250 g (9 oz) chocolate ripple or plain chocolate
   biscuits (cookies), broken into pieces

100 g (3½ oz) unsalted butter, melted

makes
12

Line a 12-hole standard muffin tin with paper cases.
Preheat the oven to 130°C (250°F/Gas 1).

To make the base, place the biscuits in the bowl of a
food processor and process to fine crumbs. Add the
butter and pulse to combine. Divide the base mixture
among the paper cases and press down firmly with a
spoon. Place in freezer for 10 minutes, or until firm.

Meanwhile, beat the sugar and cream cheese in a
large bowl using electric beaters until smooth. Add
the eggs and egg yolks, one at a time, beating well
after each addition, then stir in the sour cream and
coffee. Sift in the flour and stir until just combined.
Transfer 125 ml (4 fl oz/½ cup) of the filling to a
small bowl, then spoon the remaining filling evenly
over the base in the paper cases.

Add the melted chocolate and Kahlua to the reserved
filling and mix well. Drop teaspoons of the chocolate
mixture on top of the filling and swirl using a wooden
skewer. Bake for 30–35 minutes, or until just firm.
Allow to cool to room temperature in the tin, then
remove and serve.

Coffee swirl cheesecakes will keep well, stored in an
airtight container in the refrigerator, for up to 3 days.

Fruit tart cupcakes

185 g (6½ oz) unsalted butter, softened

170 g (6 oz/¾ cup) caster (superfine) sugar

1 teaspoon natural vanilla extract

3 eggs

125 g (4½ oz/1 cup) self-raising flour

30 g (1 oz/¼ cup) plain (all-purpose) flour

125 ml (4 fl oz/½ cup) milk

125 g (4½ oz/½ cup) thick custard

1 kiwi fruit, peeled

125 g (5 oz) strawberries

1 freestone peach, peeled

red grapes (about 4 to 6)

160 g (5⅔ oz/½ cup) apricot jam

makes
12

Preheat the oven to 180°C (350°F/Gas 4). Line 12 standard muffin holes with paper cases.

Beat butter, sugar and vanilla together with electric beaters until light and creamy. Add the eggs, one at a time, beating well after each addition. Sift the flours together and fold in alternately with the milk.

Divide the mixture evenly among the cases. Bake for 15 minutes, or until a skewer comes out clean when inserted in the centre of a cake. Transfer to a wire rack to cool.

Cut the centre out of each cake, leaving a 1 cm (½ inch) border. Fill each cavity with 2 teaspoons of custard. Cut the fruit and arrange over the custard. Heat the jam until runny. Lightly brush the jam over the top of each cake. Refrigerate until ready to serve.

Chocolate butterfly cakes

Preheat the oven to 190°C (375°F/Gas 5). Grease 18 holes of two 12-hole non-stick mini muffin tins.

Cream butter, sugar and vanilla in a medium-sized bowl using electric beaters until mixture is pale and fluffy. Add the egg and beat well. In a separate bowl, sift together the flour and cocoa. Add half the flour mixture to the butter mixture and beat until just combined. Add the milk and beat until just combined. Add the remaining flour mixture and beat until just combined.

Spoon mixture into the prepared tins. Bake for about 8 minutes, or until cooked when a skewer inserted in the centre of a cake comes out clean. Allow to stand in the tins for 2 minutes, then transfer to a wire rack to cool completely.

Cut a shallow cone-shaped piece from the top of a cooled cake. Cut the piece of cake in half to form two wedges. Fill the hollow in the centre of the cake with a little of the cream and then add a little of the jam. Lightly press the two cake wedges into the jam to form the butterfly wings. Repeat with the remaining cakes, cream and jam. Dust with the icing sugar.

These butterfly cakes are best eaten on the day they are made.

60 g (2¼ oz/¼ cup) unsalted butter, softened

80 g (2¾ oz/⅓ cup) soft brown sugar

½ teaspoon natural vanilla extract

1 egg, at room temperature

60 g (2¼ oz/½ cup) self-raising flour

30 g (1 oz/¼ cup) unsweetened cocoa powder

2 tablespoons milk

50 g (1¾ oz/¼ cup) thick (double/heavy) cream

80 g (2¾ oz/¼ cup) raspberry jam

icing (confectioners') sugar, sifted, for dusting

makes
18

TIP You can use mascarpone cheese in place of the thick cream.

Hawaiian macadamia cupcakes

185 g (6½ oz/1½ cups) self-raising flour

½ teaspoon ground cinnamon

170 g (6 oz/¾ cup) caster (superfine) sugar

45 g (1⅔ oz/½ cup) desiccated coconut

3 eggs, lightly beaten

220 g (7¾ oz) tinned crushed pineapple in syrup,
    drained

185 ml (6 fl oz/¾ cup) vegetable oil

50 g (1¾ oz) macadamia nuts, chopped, plus extra
    to decorate

Lemon cream

90 g (3¼ oz) cream cheese, softened

45 g (1½ oz) unsalted butter, softened

1½ tablespoons lemon juice

280 g (10 oz/2¼ cups) icing (confectioners') sugar,
    sifted

makes
18

Preheat the oven to 180°C (350°F/Gas 4).
Line 18 standard muffin holes with paper cases.

Sift the flour and cinnamon into a large bowl, then add the sugar and coconut and stir to combine. Add the egg, pineapple and oil and mix well. Stir in the macadamia nuts.

Divide the mixture evenly among the cases. Bake for 18–20 minutes, or until a skewer comes out clean when inserted in the centre of a cake. Transfer to a wire rack to cool.

To make the lemon cream, beat the cream cheese and butter in a large bowl with electric beaters until smooth. Add the lemon juice and icing sugar, and beat until well combined.

Decorate each cake with lemon cream and a sprinkling of macadamia nuts.

Mandarin and chamomile cupcakes

185 ml (6 fl oz/¾ cup) milk

5 g (⅛ oz/¼ cup) chamomile tea flowers, plus extra to decorate

150 g (5½ oz) unsalted butter, chopped

230 g (8½ oz/1 cup) caster (superfine) sugar

3 eggs

2 teaspoons finely grated mandarin zest

300 g (10½ oz) mandarin, peeled, seeds removed

60 g (2¼ oz/½ cup) fine semolina

155 g (5⅔ oz/1¼ cups) self-raising flour

Mandarin glaze

155 g (5½ oz/1¼ cups) icing (confectioners') sugar, sifted

1 teaspoon finely grated mandarin zest

2–3 tablespoons strained, fresh mandarin juice

chamomile tea flowers, to garnish

makes
20

Preheat the oven to 180°C (350°F/Gas 4). Line 20 mini muffin holes with paper cases.

Place the milk and chamomile tea flowers into a saucepan and bring just to the boil. Stand for 5 minutes to infuse. Strain.

Place the butter, sugar, eggs, mandarin zest and mandarin in a food processor and process until almost smooth. Add the milk mixture, semolina and flour and process until smooth. Pour mixture evenly among the cases. Bake for 8–10 minutes, or until a skewer comes out clean when inserted in the centre of a cake. Transfer to a wire rack to cool.

To make the mandarin glaze, place the icing sugar, zest and enough juice to make a paste in a heatproof bowl. Sit the bowl over a pan of simmering water, making sure the base of the bowl doesn't touch the water, and stir until runny. Remove from the heat but keep the bowl over the water. Spread the glaze over each cake and decorate with a chamomile flower.

high tea

Bite-sized bliss

Rosewater meringues with raspberry cream

4 egg whites

230 g (8¼ oz/1 cup) caster (superfine) sugar

1 tablespoon rosewater

few drops of pink food colouring (optional)

sugared rose petals (optional)

2–3 unsprayed pink or red roses

1 egg white, lightly beaten

115 g (4 oz/½ cup) caster (superfine) sugar

Raspberry cream

300 ml (10½ fl oz) thick (double/heavy) cream

1 tablespoon icing (confectioners') sugar, sifted

100 g (3½ oz) fresh raspberries or thawed frozen
    raspberries

makes
30

Preheat the oven to 120°C (235°F/Gas ½). Line two baking trays with baking paper and mark 30, 3 cm (1¼ inch) rounds on each sheet of paper.

Beat the egg whites in a large bowl with electric beaters until stiff peaks form. Add sugar gradually, beating well after each addition, and continue to beat until the mixture is thick and glossy. Add rosewater and food colouring, if using, to tint the meringue pale pink. Transfer the mixture, in batches if necessary, to a piping (icing) bag fitted with a 1 cm (½ inch) plain nozzle. Following the marked rounds as a guide, pipe 60 rounds, about 2 cm (¾ inch) high, onto the paper. Bake for 1 hour. Leave to cool in the oven with the door slightly open.

To make the sugared rose petals, if using, remove the petals from the roses. Use a small paintbrush to lightly brush the egg white over both sides of each petal. Toss lightly in the sugar and set aside to dry. Repeat with the remaining petals.

To make the raspberry cream, beat the cream and sugar until thick, fold in the raspberries. Spread the raspberry cream over the base of half the meringues, sandwich with the remaining meringues and decorate with the sugared rose petals, if using.

Unfilled meringues will keep, stored in an airtight container in a cool place, for up to 2 weeks.

Mini cherry galettes

670 g (1 lb 7½ oz) jar pitted morello cherries,
   drained

30 g (1 oz) unsalted butter

1½ tablespoons caster (superfine) sugar

1 egg yolk

½ teaspoon natural vanilla extract

55 g (2 oz/½ cup) ground almonds

1 tablespoon plain (all-purpose) flour

2 sheets ready-rolled puff pastry

icing (confectioners') sugar, sifted, for dusting

160 g (5¾ oz/½ cup) cherry jam, melted

makes
30

Preheat the oven to 180°C (350°F/Gas 4). Line a baking tray with baking paper.

Spread the cherries on several sheets of paper towel to absorb any excess liquid.

Combine the butter and caster sugar in a medium bowl and beat until pale and fluffy. Add the egg yolk and vanilla, then stir in the combined ground almonds and flour. Refrigerate until required.

Cut 30 rounds from the pastry sheets using a 5 cm (2 inch) cutter. Place half the rounds on the prepared tray and lightly prick all over with a fork. Cover with another sheet of baking paper and weigh down with another baking tray—this prevents the pastry from rising during cooking. Bake for 10 minutes, remove from the oven and allow to cool on the tray. Repeat with the remaining rounds.

Spread level ½ teaspoons of the almond mixture over each cooled pastry round, then press three cherries onto the almond mixture. Bake for 10 minutes, or until lightly browned. Cool slightly and dust lightly with the icing sugar. Glaze the cherries by drizzling them with the warmed jam.

NOTE The almond topping can be prepared up to 4 days in advance. Assemble the cherry galettes on the day they are to be eaten so that the pastry base doesn't go soggy.

Brandy snap flowers

Preheat the oven to 180°C (350°F/Gas 4). Lightly grease two baking trays.

Place the butter, sugar, golden syrup, chicory essence, coffee and brandy in a small saucepan. Stir over low heat until the butter melts and the sugar dissolves. Remove from the heat and stir in the flour and ginger.

Drop ¼ teaspoons of the mixture well apart onto the prepared trays (only cook a maximum of four biscuits per tray). Bake for 3–4 minutes, or until golden. Be careful not to allow the brandy snaps to burn. Leave for 1–2 minutes, then press into the base of muffin mini tins to curl the brandy snaps. Set aside.

If using the melted chocolate, drizzle the chocolate over the base of the brandy snaps and allow to set.

Brandy snaps will keep, stored in an airtight container, for 2–3 days.

50 g (1¾ oz) unsalted butter

55 g (2 oz/¼ cup) soft brown sugar

1 tablespoon golden syrup (light treacle)

1 teaspoon chicory essence (camp coffee)

½ teaspoon instant coffee powder

2 teaspoons brandy

40 g (1½ oz/1⅓ cup) plain (all-purpose) flour

1 teaspoon ground ginger

200 g (7 oz) dark chocolate, melted (optional)

makes
88

Mini raspberry and frangipane tarts

125 g (4½ oz/½ cup) unsalted butter, chilled and
    cut into cubes

155 g (5½ oz/1¼ cups) plain (all-purpose) flour

55 g (2 oz) icing (confectioners') sugar, plus extra,
    sifted, for dusting (optional)

1 large egg yolk

120 g (4¼ oz) raspberries

Filling

55 g (2 oz/¼ cup) sugar

60 g (2¼ oz/¼ cup) unsalted butter, softened

1 large egg

1 teaspoon natural vanilla extract

55 g (2 oz/½ cup) ground almonds

1 tablespoon plain (all-purpose) flour

60 g (2¼ oz) white chocolate, roughly chopped

makes
24

Place the butter and flour in the bowl of a food processor and process until fine breadcrumbs form. Add the sugar and egg yolk and process until the dough just comes together, adding ½ tablespoon iced water, if necessary. Turn out onto a lightly floured work surface and gather into a ball. Wrap in plastic wrap and refrigerate for 30 minutes.

Meanwhile, preheat the oven to 180°C (350°F/Gas 4). Lightly grease 24, 5 cm (2 inch) fluted mini tartlet tins or two 12-hole mini muffin tins.

Divide the pastry in half. Roll out each piece between two sheets of baking paper until 2 mm (⅟₁₆ inch) thick, scattering with flour where necessary. Cut out 24 rounds from the pastry with a 6 cm (2½ inch) cutter. Line each prepared tin with a circle of pastry and trim off any excess. Prick the bases with a fork. Place in the freezer for 5 minutes. Line the bases with baking paper, pour in some baking beads or uncooked rice and bake for 5 minutes. Remove the paper and beads and bake for another 2–3 minutes, or until just golden. Set aside to cool.

To make filling, beat sugar and butter in a medium bowl using electric beaters for 30 seconds. Add egg and vanilla and beat for another 30 seconds. Fold in ground almonds, flour and chocolate. Spoon filling into the pastry cases. Press a raspberry into the top of each tart. Bake for 8–10 minutes, or until filling is golden and set. Remove from tins by turning upside down and tapping with the back of a knife handle. Dust tarts with extra icing sugar, if desired.

Coffee and sugar crystal meringues

2 egg whites

145 g (5¼ oz/⅔ cup) caster (superfine) sugar

1 teaspoon instant coffee powder

1 tablespoon icing (confectioners') sugar

40 g (1½ oz/⅓ cup) chopped walnuts

2 tablespoons coffee sugar crystals

makes
40

Preheat the oven to 120°C (235°F/Gas ½). Line two baking trays with baking paper.

Beat the egg whites in a bowl with electric beaters until stiff peaks form. Gradually add the caster sugar, beating continuously, until the sugar is dissolved and the mixture is thick and glossy.

Beat in the coffee powder until the mixture is slightly coloured. Sift the icing sugar and quickly fold into the mixture with the walnuts. Drop rounded teaspoons of the mixture well apart, to allow for spreading, onto the prepared trays.

Sprinkle with the coffee sugar crystals and bake for 25 minutes, or until crisp and dry. Turn off the oven and leave the meringues to cool completely in the oven with the door ajar.

NOTE It is best to chop the walnuts by hand.

Chocolate fruit and nut clusters

Line two baking trays with baking paper.

Place each type of chocolate in separate heatproof bowls over saucepans of simmering water, ensuring the bowls don't touch the water. Stir until chocolate has melted and is smooth. Remove from the heat.

Combine the nuts and dried fruits in a bowl. Stir half into each type of chocolate, mixing thoroughly. Set aside for 10 minutes to allow the chocolate to firm a little. Put small heaped spoonfuls onto the prepared trays. Refrigerate until firm.

The clusters will keep stored in an airtight container, for up to 2 weeks.

NOTE Sweetened dried cranberries are sometimes sold as craisins.

125 g (4½ oz) milk chocolate, chopped

125 g (4½ oz) dark chocolate, chopped

80 g (2¾ oz/½ cup) toasted unsalted macadamia nuts, quartered

70 g (2½ oz/½ cup) toasted skinned hazelnuts, halved

75 g (2½ oz/⅓ cup) glacé (candied) ginger pieces, chopped

60 g (2¼ oz/⅓ cup) dried apricots, chopped

40 g (1½ oz/⅓ cup) sweetened dried cranberries (see Note)

makes
40

Mini profiteroles

60 g (2¼ oz/¼ cup) unsalted butter, chopped

250 ml (9 fl oz/1 cup) water

125 g (4½ oz/1 cup) plain (all-purpose) flour, sifted

4 eggs, beaten

300 ml (10½ fl oz) whipping cream

1 tablespoon icing (confectioners') sugar, sifted

½ teaspoon natural vanilla extract

50 g (1¾ oz) dark chocolate, melted

makes
48

Preheat the oven to 200°C (400°F/Gas 6) and line two baking trays with baking paper.

Place the butter and water in a saucepan and stir over low heat until the butter melts. Bring to the boil, remove from the heat and add all the flour. Beat with a wooden spoon until smooth. Return to the heat and beat for 2 minutes, or until the mixture forms a ball and leaves the side of the pan. Remove from the heat and transfer to a bowl. Cool for 5 minutes. Add the egg, a little at a time, beating well after each addition, and continue beating until thick and glossy—a wooden spoon should stand upright in the mixture.

Spoon the mixture into a piping (icing) bag with a 1 cm (½ inch) fluted nozzle. Pipe 3 cm (1¼ inch) rounds of batter onto the prepared trays. Bake for 10 minutes, then reduce the heat to 180°C (350°F/Gas 4) and cook for a further 10 minutes, or until golden and puffed. Poke a hole in one side of each profiterole and remove the soft dough from inside with a teaspoon. Return the profiteroles to the oven for 2–3 minutes. Cool on a wire rack.

Whip the cream, sugar and vanilla until thick. Pipe the cream into the side of each profiterole. Dip each profiterole in the melted chocolate, face side down, then return to the wire rack for the chocolate to set.

Hazelnut brittle

Line a 30 x 25 cm (12 x 10 inch) baking tray with baking paper.

Combine the sugar and water in a small heavy-based saucepan over medium–high heat and stir well until sugar has dissolved. Cook without stirring, brushing down the sides with a pastry brush if necessary, for 10–12 minutes, or until golden. Quickly add the hazelnuts and zest; stir to combine. Pour immediately onto the prepared baking tray, spreading to cover the whole surface. Allow to cool.

Break into bite-sized pieces. Store in an airtight container.

NOTE Toast hazelnuts in a 180°C (350°F/Gas 4) oven for 5–10 minutes, or until lightly golden. Tip the nuts onto a clean tea towel (dish towel) and rub gently to remove the skins.

220 g (7¾ oz/1 cup) sugar
125 ml (4 fl oz/½ cup) water
35 g (1¼ oz/¼ cup) hazelnuts, lightly toasted, skinned and roughly chopped
finely grated zest of 1 orange

makes
24

Nutty chocolate fudge

370 g (13 oz/2 cups) raw caster (superfine) sugar

170 ml (5½ fl oz/⅔ cup) evaporated milk

20 g (¾ oz) unsalted butter

100 g (3½ oz) white marshmallows

250 g (9 oz/1⅔ cups) chopped dark chocolate

125 g (4½ oz) unsalted mixed nuts, toasted, roughly
    chopped

60 g (2¼ oz) white chocolate, chopped

makes
48

Grease an 18 cm (7 inch) square baking tin and line with baking paper, extending the paper over two opposite sides for easy removal later.

Combine the sugar, evaporated milk and butter in a saucepan over low heat and cook until the sugar dissolves. Increase the heat to medium, bring to the boil and simmer, stirring, for 4–5 minutes. Remove from the heat and stir in the marshmallows and dark chocolate. Continue stirring until smooth, then add the nuts. Pour into the prepared tin and refrigerate until set.

Melt the white chocolate in a heatproof bowl over a saucepan of simmering water, ensuring that the bowl doesn't touch the water.

Remove the chocolate nut mixture from the tin and cut into 1.5 x 4.5 cm (⅝ x 1¾ inch) pieces. Place the pieces on a sheet of baking paper, and use a piping (icing) bag to pipe the white chocolate in drizzly lines over the top. Leave the white chocolate to set before storing or eating.

Store fudge in an airtight container in the refrigerator. When ready to eat, remove from the refrigerator and leave at room temperature for 10 minutes to allow the fudge to soften slightly.

Mini lime meringue pies

4 sheets ready-rolled sweet shortcrust pastry

115 g (4 oz/½ cup) caster (superfine) sugar

30 g (1 oz/¼ cup) cornflour (cornstarch)

2 teaspoons finely grated lime zest

80 ml (2½ fl oz/⅓ cup) lime juice

185 ml (6 fl oz/¾ cup) water

30 g (1 oz) unsalted butter

2 egg yolks

Meringue

3 egg whites

170 g (6 oz/¾ cup) caster (superfine) sugar

makes
24

Preheat the oven to 180°C (350°F/Gas 4). Grease two 12-hole mini muffin tins.

Use a 7 cm (2¾ inch) cutter to cut 24 rounds from the pastry sheets. Press the rounds into the prepared tins and prick the bases well with a fork. Bake for 12–15 minutes, or until golden brown. Set aside to cool.

Combine the sugar, cornflour, lime zest and juice, and water in a large saucepan and stir over medium heat until the mixture boils and thickens. Remove from the heat and add the butter. Mix well and gradually stir in the egg yolks. Spoon 1 heaped teaspoon of the lime curd into each pastry case.

To make the meringue, beat the egg whites in a large bowl with electric beaters until stiff peaks form. Gradually add sugar, beating until it dissolves and the mixture is thick and glossy. Spoon 1 tablespoon of meringue over each pie. Bake for 4–5 minutes, or until lightly golden on top.

These pies will keep, stored in an airtight container, for up to 2 days.

Mini mud cakes

170 g (6 oz/¾ cup) caster (superfine) sugar

175 g (6 oz) dark chocolate, chopped

90 g (3¼ oz/⅓ cup) unsalted butter, chopped

60 ml (2 fl oz/¼ cup) water

2 eggs, lightly beaten

2 tablespoons brandy

60 g (2¼ oz/½ cup) plain (all-purpose) flour

60 g (2¼ oz/½ cup) self-raising flour

30 g (1 oz/¼ cup) unsweetened cocoa powder

Chocolate curls

50 g (1¾ oz/⅓ cup) milk chocolate melts (buttons)

Ganache

200 g (7 oz/1⅓ cups) dark chocolate melts
    (buttons), chopped

125 ml (4 fl oz/½ cup) cream

makes
30

Preheat the oven to 180°C (350°F/Gas 4). Lightly grease base and sides of a 20 x 30 cm (8 x 12 inch) baking tin. Cover the base and two long sides with baking paper.

Place the sugar, chocolate, butter and water in a small saucepan and stir over low heat for 5 minutes, or until chocolate melts. Remove from the heat, cool to room temperature then stir in the egg and brandy.

Sift the flours and cocoa into a bowl and make a well in the centre. Pour the chocolate mixture into the well. Mix well and pour into the prepared tin. Bake for 20–25 minutes, or until a skewer inserted in the centre comes out clean. Cool in the tin for 5 minutes before inverting onto a wire rack to cool completely.

Dip a 3 cm (1¼ inch) cookie cutter in hot water and cut out 30 rounds from the cake, re-dipping the cutter between each round (this produces a neater edge). Roll the cut surface gently on the bench to press in any crumbs. Place the mini cakes, top side down, on a wire rack over a baking tray.

To make the chocolate curls, place the chocolate melts in a heatproof bowl. Half-fill a saucepan with water, bring to the boil and remove from the heat. Sit the bowl over the saucepan, ensuring the bowl doesn't touch the water. Stir occasionally until the chocolate has melted. Spread the chocolate fairly thinly over a marble board or a cool baking tray and leave at room temperature until just set. Using the edge of a sharp knife at a 45 degree angle, scrape over the top of the chocolate. The chocolate strips will curl as they come away—don't press too hard. If the chocolate has set too firmly, the curls will break. If so, leave in a warm place and try again.

To make the ganache, place the chocolate melts in a bowl. Heat the cream in a saucepan until almost boiling, pour over the chocolate and leave for 2 minutes, then stir until the chocolate has melted and is smooth. Spoon the chocolate ganache evenly over the cakes, reheating if too thick. Tap the tray gently to settle the chocolate, top each cake with a chocolate curl and allow to set. Use a spatula to remove the cakes from the wire rack. (For image, see page 68.)

Crème caramel petits fours

200 ml (7 fl oz) milk

145 ml (4¾ fl oz) pouring cream

1 vanilla bean, split lengthways and seeds scraped

40 g (1½ oz) caster (superfine) sugar

2 large eggs

250 ml (9 fl oz/1 cup) cream, whipped to
  soft peaks

Pastry

125 g (4½ oz/½ cup) unsalted butter, chilled and
  cut into cubes

155 g (5½ oz/1¼ cups) plain (all-purpose) flour

60 g (2¼ oz/½ cup) icing (confectioners') sugar,
  plus extra, sifted, for dusting

1 large egg yolk

Caramel

100 g (3½ oz) caster (superfine) sugar

60 ml (2 fl oz/¼ cup) water

makes
24

To make the pastry, place the butter and flour in the bowl of a food processor and process until the mixture is the consistency of fine breadcrumbs. Add the sugar and egg yolk and process until the dough just comes together, adding ½ tablespoon of iced water, if necessary. Turn out onto a lightly floured work surface and gather into a ball. Wrap in plastic wrap and refrigerate for 30 minutes.

Preheat the oven to 180°C (350°F/Gas 4). Lightly grease two 12-hole mini muffin tins.

Slice the pastry in half. Roll out each piece between two sheets of baking paper until 2 mm (1/16 inch) thick, scattering with flour where necessary. Use a 6 cm (2½ inch) cutter to cut out 24 rounds. Line each prepared tin with a pastry round and trim off any excess. Prick bases with a fork. Place in the freezer for 5 minutes. Line bases with baking paper and pour in some baking beads or uncooked rice. Bake for about 6 minutes. Remove the paper and beads and bake for 3–5 minutes, or until just golden. Allow to cool.

Reduce oven temperature to 160°C (315°F/Gas 2–3). Grease 24 mini baba tins.

To make the caramel, place the sugar and 45 ml (1½ fl oz) water in a heavy-based saucepan. Bring to the boil, stirring to dissolve the sugar, reduce the heat and simmer, without stirring, for 5–7 minutes, or until golden. Brush any sugar on the side of the pan with a wet pastry brush to avoid crystallising. Do not overcook or the toffee will taste burnt. Very carefully add the remaining water to stop the caramel cooking. (Stand back as the caramel will spit.) Quickly spoon a little of the caramel into the base of each mould before it sets.

Combine the milk, cream and vanilla seeds in a medium saucepan and bring to just below boiling point. Remove from the heat. Whisk the sugar and eggs in a bowl until light and creamy. Pour in the hot milk mixture. Strain through a sieve and remove any excess froth with a spoon. Pour into the prepared baba moulds. Stand the moulds in a large baking tin and pour in hot water to come halfway up the sides of the moulds. Bake for 15 minutes, or until custard is set. Remove the crème caramels from the water bath and allow to sit for 5 minutes. Then transfer to the refrigerator to chill for 30 minutes.

Pipe or spoon a generous swirl of cream into each tart case. Invert the crème caramels over the tart cases, breaking the seal with a sharp, thin knife. Spoon over any extra caramel. Serve immediately.

NOTE The pastry cases and the crème caramel can be prepared ahead of time, but the petits fours should not be assembled until just before serving as the pastry will become soft. (For image, see page 69.)

Sesame and ginger wafers

40 g (1½ oz) unsalted butter

40 g (1½ oz) caster (superfine) sugar

2 tablespoons golden syrup (light treacle)
   or dark corn syrup

40 g (1½ oz/⅓ cup) plain (all-purpose) flour

½ teaspoon ground ginger

1 tablespoon brandy

2 teaspoons lemon juice

1 tablespoon sesame seeds, toasted

makes
36

Preheat the oven to 190°C (375°F/Gas 5). Grease two baking trays.

Combine the butter, sugar and syrup in a small saucepan and heat gently, stirring occasionally, until the butter melts and the mixture is smooth. Remove from the heat.

Sift the flour and ginger into a bowl. Add the melted butter mixture and the brandy, lemon juice and sesame seeds and stir to mix well.

Drop ½ teaspoons of the mixture onto the prepared trays (only cook four wafers per tray), leaving enough room to allow for spreading. Use a spatula to spread each wafer out to form a 5 cm (2 inch) round. Bake for 3–4 minutes, or until the wafers begin to brown around the edges. Cool for 1 minute. Using a palette knife and working quickly, carefully remove the warm biscuits from the trays, then quickly drape them over the handle of a wooden spoon to make them curl. Cool completely, then remove from the wooden spoon. Repeat with the remaining mixture.

Sesame and ginger wafers are best eaten on the day they are made.

Baileys and white chocolate opera

Line two baking trays with baking paper. To make the Baileys butter cream, place the chocolate in a heatproof bowl. Half-fill a saucepan with water and bring to the boil. Sit the bowl over the saucepan, making sure the base of the bowl does not touch the water. Stir occasionally until melted. Cream the butter and sugar in a small bowl until light and fluffy. Add the Baileys and chocolate and beat until smooth.

Trim the sponges to 3 cm (1¼ inches) in thickness. Slice each sponge into three horizontal layers. Place the first layer on one side of a prepared tray and spread with one-quarter of the butter cream. Repeat with the second layer and another quarter of the butter cream. Top with the last layer of cake. Repeat on the other side of the tray with the other cake and butter cream, reserving enough cream for the tops, and place both cakes in the freezer for 20 minutes, or until firm. Cut each cake into 12 squares.

Lightly beat the egg white in a small bowl. Pierce a blueberry with a skewer, dip into the egg white and sprinkle with the sugar. Transfer to a plate. Repeat with the remaining blueberries and set aside.

Pour the melted chocolate onto the remaining prepared tray. Spread to a thickness of 2 mm (1/16 inch). Allow to set, them cut into 24 squares the same size as the petits fours. Spread a small amount of the butter cream on top of each petit four and top with the chocolate. Place butter cream in the centre of each and top with a blueberry.

two 14 x 20 cm (5½ x 8 inch) ready-made sponge
   cakes
1 egg white
24 blueberries
115 g (4 oz/½ cup) caster (superfine) sugar
100 g (3½ oz) white chocolate, melted

Baileys butter cream
250 g (9 oz) white chocolate, chopped
185 g (6½ oz/¾ cup) unsalted butter, softened
30 g (1 oz/¼ cup) icing (confectioners') sugar
2½ tablespoons Baileys Irish Cream

makes
24

Raspberry and coconut ice petits fours

150 g (5½ oz) white chocolate, chopped

Coconut ice

125 g (4½ oz/1 cup) icing (confectioners') sugar

80 ml (2½ fl oz/⅓ cup) sweetened
   condensed milk

45g (1²/³ oz/½ cup) desiccated coconut

20 g (¾ oz) Copha (white vegetable
   shortening), melted

1 small egg white

Sugar-coated raspberries

1 small egg white

125 g (4½ oz/1 cup) raspberries

55 g (2 oz/¼ cup) caster (superfine) sugar

makes
12

Place the chocolate in a heatproof bowl over a saucepan of simmering water, ensuring that the bowl doesn't touch the water. Stir until the chocolate has melted. Paint the inside of 12 small paper cases evenly with half the chocolate. Place on a baking tray and transfer to the freezer until set. Paint again carefully with the remaining chocolate. Return to the freezer until set. Carefully peel off the paper cases.

To make the coconut ice, sift the sugar into a bowl. Add the condensed milk, coconut and Copha and stir until well combined. In a separate, clean bowl, beat the egg white until soft peaks form. Fold into the coconut mixture. Spoon the coconut ice into the chocolate cases and press it flat with a teaspoon dipped in boiling water. Refrigerate until needed.

To make sugar-coated raspberries, lightly whisk the egg white. Place a raspberry on a skewer, dip it into the egg white and sprinkle with sugar. Repeat with the remaining raspberries. Transfer to a plate lined with paper towels and allow to set.

Top each petit four with a sugar-coated raspberry and refrigerate until needed. These petits fours will freeze well.

Lavender and honey madeleines

30 g (1 oz) unsalted butter

2 teaspoons honey

2½ tablespoons caster (superfine) sugar

½ teaspoon dried lavender

30 g (1 oz/¼ cup) plain (all-purpose) flour

1½ tablespoons ground almonds

1 large egg, at room temperature

1 tablespoon icing (confectioners') sugar, sifted,
    for dusting (optional)

makes
30

Preheat oven to 180°C (350°F/Gas 4). Use a pastry brush to lightly grease 30 mini madeleine moulds.

Melt the butter and honey in a small saucepan over a medium heat. Set aside to cool. Place the caster sugar and lavender in the bowl of a food processor and process until combined. Sift the flour, ground almonds and a pinch of salt three times onto baking paper. (This will lighten the madeleines' texture.)

Beat the egg and sugar mixture in a bowl with electric beaters until thick and creamy. Add the flour mixture and the cooled butter mixture and fold in lightly with a metal spoon until just combined. Allow to stand for 10 minutes. Spoon into the prepared madeleine moulds until three-quarters full. Bake for 6–8 minutes, or until lightly golden. Carefully remove from the moulds and place on a wire rack to cool. Dust lightly with icing sugar before serving.

Madeleines should be eaten the same day that they are baked.

White chocolate bark

Preheat the oven to 180°C (350°F/Gas 4) and line a baking tray with baking paper.

Spread the nuts over a second baking tray and toast for 5–6 minutes, or until lightly browned, shaking the tray once or twice to ensure even toasting. Cool.

Place the chocolate in a heatproof bowl over a saucepan of simmering water, ensuring the bowl doesn't touch the water. Stir until chocolate is just melted and smooth. Remove from the heat, then add two-thirds of the nuts and dried fruit and stir to coat.

Pour the mixture onto the prepared tray and spread to form approximately a square of 25 cm (10 inches). Scatter over the remaining nuts and dried fruit. Cover with plastic wrap and refrigerate until set.

Break into small chunks and store, in an airtight container, in the refrigerator for 3 weeks.

160 g (5¾ oz/1 cup) unsalted macadamia nuts, chopped
225 g (8 oz/1⅔ cups) chopped white chocolate
120 g (4¼ oz/⅔ cup) dried apricots, finely chopped
50 g (1¾ oz/⅓ cup) currants

makes
8–10

Mini rum babas

1 egg, separated

55 g (2 oz/¼ cup) caster (superfine) sugar

¼ teaspoon natural vanilla extract

60 g (2¼ oz/½ cup) self-raising flour

30 g (1 oz) unsalted butter

30 ml (1 fl oz) milk

whipped cream, to serve

Sauce

170 g (6 oz/¾ cup) caster (superfine) sugar

185 ml (6 fl oz/¾ cup) rum

80 ml (2½ fl oz/⅓ cup) fresh orange juice, strained

80 ml (2½ fl oz/⅓ cup) fresh lime juice, strained

3 x 5 cm (2 inch) pieces orange zest

makes
36

To make the sauce, combine all the ingredients in a small saucepan over medium–high heat, stirring to dissolve the sugar. Bring to the boil, reduce heat to medium and simmer, without stirring, for 8 minutes, or until golden and syrupy, brushing the sugar from the side of the pan with a wet pastry brush as necessary. Remove the zest and slice very finely.

Preheat the oven to 170°C (325°F/Gas 3). Lightly spray 36 mini baba tins with oil.

Beat the egg white and a pinch of salt in a clean bowl until soft peaks form. Gradually add the sugar, and beat until thick and glossy and sugar has dissolved. Add the egg yolk and vanilla and beat again.

Sift the flour onto baking paper three times. Heat the butter and milk in a small saucepan over medium heat until the butter has melted. Gently fold the flour and butter mixture into the egg mixture. Spoon into the prepared tins. Place on a baking tray and bake for 6–8 minutes, or until just starting to colour. Do not overcook. Carefully remove from the tins, while still warm and place on a serving plate.

Spoon over the warm sauce until the babas are well soaked. Spoon or pipe the cream onto the top of each rum baba. Garnish with slivers of orange zest and serve warm or cold.

Homemade chocolate freckles

150 g (5½ oz) milk chocolate melts (buttons)
ready-made sprinkles of your choice (such as
    hundreds and thousands, silver or mixed cachous
    and/or coloured sprinkles)

makes
12

Line a large tray with baking paper.

Place chocolate in a heatproof bowl over a saucepan of simmering water, ensuring the bowl doesn't touch the water. Stir until chocolate has melted. Remove from the heat.

Working with 2 teaspoons of the chocolate at a time, shape into 12 rounds on the prepared tray 5 cm (2 inches) apart. Lightly tap the tray on the bench to spread the chocolate out to form 5 cm (2 inch) discs. Top the chocolate discs with the sprinkles of your choice. Stand at room temperature for 30 minutes, or until set.

The chocolate freckles will keep, stored in an airtight container in a cool place, for up to 2 weeks.

Apricot ricotta tarts with coffee crème fraîche

175 g (6 oz) ricotta cheese

125 g (4½ oz/½ cup) unsalted butter, softened

90 g (3¼ oz/½ cup) raw caster (superfine) sugar

3 eggs, separated

finely grated zest and juice of 1 orange

100 g (3½ oz) ground hazelnuts

75 g (2¾ oz) plain (all-purpose) flour

6 firm ripe apricots, halved and stones removed

Coffee crème fraîche

200 g (7 oz) crème fraîche

30 g (1 oz/¼ cup) icing (confectioners') sugar

1 tablespoon freshly made espresso coffee, cooled

makes
24

To make coffee crème fraîche, place crème fraîche in a bowl, sift in the sugar and stir to combine. Stir in the coffee, cover with plastic wrap and place in the refrigerator until required.

Preheat the oven to 180°C (350°F/Gas 4). Grease 2 x 12-hole standard muffin tins and line each base with baking paper.

Use the back of a spoon to push the ricotta through a sieve over a bowl.

Cream the butter and sugar in a bowl using electric beaters until pale and fluffy. Add the egg yolks, one at a time, beating well after each addition. Stir in the ricotta, orange zest and juice. Fold in the combined ground hazelnuts and flour. Beat the egg whites in a separate bowl until stiff peaks form and fold into the ricotta mixture. Spoon the batter into the prepared tin and smooth the surface with the back of a spoon. Place an apricot half, skin side down, on top of batter. Bake for 12–15 minutes, or until cooked through.

Serve hot with a dollop of the coffee crème fraîche.

VARIATION Replace the apricots with plums or raspberries.

Chewy caramel walnut bites

125 g (4½ oz/½ cup) unsalted butter, cut into
  cubes
400 g (14 oz) tin sweetened condensed milk
2 tablespoons golden syrup (light treacle)
165 g (5¾ oz/¾ cup) soft brown sugar
100 g (3½ oz/1 cup) walnut halves, toasted, finely
  chopped, plus extra, to decorate
400 g (14 oz/2⅔ cups) chopped dark chocolate

makes
54

Grease an 18 cm (7 inch) square baking tin and line with baking paper, extending the paper over two opposite sides for easy removal later. Line a baking tray with baking paper.

Combine the butter, condensed milk, golden syrup and sugar in a saucepan and stir over low heat until the butter melts and the sugar dissolves. Increase the heat a little so that the mixture bubbles at a steady slow boil. Stir constantly for 9–10 minutes, or until caramel in colour and the mixture leaves the side of the pan when stirred. Stir in the walnuts. Pour into the prepared tin. Leave at room temperature to set.

Remove from the tin, using the paper as handles. Cut into six even pieces. Gently roll each piece into a log approximately 18 cm (7 inches) long and place on the prepared tray. Refrigerate for 1 hour, or until firm. Cut each log into 2 cm (¾ inch) pieces.

Meanwhile, melt the chocolate in a heatproof bowl over a saucepan of simmering water, ensuring that the bowl doesn't touch the water. Coat each caramel log with chocolate, decorate with extra walnuts and return to the tray. Transfer to the refrigerator to set.

Refrigerate in an airtight container for up to 1 week.

Petits pithiviers

3 sheets ready-rolled puff pastry
1 egg, lightly beaten

Almond filling
40 g (1½ oz) butter, softened
40 g (1½ oz/⅓ cup) icing (confectioners') sugar
1 egg yolk
70 g (2½ oz/⅔ cup) ground almonds
1 teaspoon finely grated orange zest
few drops of natural almond extract

makes
24

Lightly grease two baking trays.

To make the almond filling, cream butter and sugar with electric beaters until pale and fluffy. Add the egg yolk and beat well. Stir in the ground almonds, orange zest and almond extract.

Lay the puff pastry on a work surface and cut into 48 rounds with a 5 cm (2 inch) cutter. Place about 1½ teaspoons of almond filling on half the rounds, leaving a 5 mm (¼ inch) border. Brush the border with beaten egg. Put the remaining pastry rounds over the filling and press the edges firmly to seal. Transfer to the prepared trays and refrigerate for 30 minutes.

Preheat the oven to 210°C (415°F/Gas 6–7).

With a blunt-edged knife, gently press up the pastry edges at intervals. Carefully score pastry tops into wedges, then brush with the remaining beaten egg.

Bake for 10 minutes, or until lightly golden.

Chocolate-dipped strawberries

Line a baking tray with baking paper.

Melt the dark chocolate in a small heatproof bowl over a saucepan of simmering water, making sure the bowl does not touch the water. Dip the bottom half of each strawberry in the chocolate, transfer to the prepared baking tray and leave to set.

When set, melt white chocolate in a small heatproof bowl over a saucepan of simmering water, making sure the base of the bowl does not touch the water. Dip the tips of the strawberries in the chocolate. Return to the baking tray and allow to set.

12 large strawberries
150 g (5½ oz) good-quality dark chocolate, roughly
   chopped
100 g (3½ oz) good-quality white chocolate,
   roughly chopped

makes
12

Black forest gâteau petits fours

455 ml (16 fl oz) cream

2 tablespoons icing (confectioners') sugar

45 ml (1½ fl oz) dark rum

200 g (7 oz/1 cup) morello cherries, drained and
    finely chopped

100 g (3½ oz) dark chocolate, grated

48 maraschino cherries, with stalks intact

Sponge

125 g (4½ oz/1 cup) plain (all-purpose) flour

2 teaspoons baking powder

60 g (2¼ oz/½ cup) unsweetened cocoa powder

125 g (4½ oz/½ cup) unsalted butter, softened

230 g (8¼ oz/1 cup) caster (superfine) sugar

4 eggs, separated

1 teaspoon natural vanilla extract

170 ml (5½ fl oz/⅔ cup) milk

makes
48

Preheat the oven to 180°C (350°F/Gas 4). Grease a 20 x 30 cm (8 x 12 inch) baking tin and line with baking paper. Line a baking tray with baking paper.

Sift the flour, baking powder and cocoa. Cream the butter and 145 g (5¼ oz/⅔ cup) sugar until pale and fluffy. Beat in the egg yolks and the vanilla. Fold in the flour mixture and the milk. Beat the egg whites in a clean bowl using electric beaters until light and foamy. Add the remaining sugar to the egg whites and beat until soft peaks form. Stir a tablespoon of the whisked egg white into the sponge mixture, then gently fold in the rest. Pour the mixture into the prepared tin and bake for 25–30 minutes or until firm. Allow to cool for 5 minutes before turning out onto a wire rack.

Beat the cream, sugar and rum in a bowl using electric beaters until firm peaks form. Remove one-third of the cream, cover with plastic wrap and refrigerate. Gently fold the morello cherries through the remaining cream.

Slice the sponge horizontally into three layers. Place the first layer on the prepared baking tray and spread with half the cherries and cream mixture. Top with another layer of sponge, and the remaining cherries and cream mixture. Finish with the remaining slice of sponge and refrigerate for 2 hours, or until firm.

Cut sponge into 3 cm (1¼ inch) squares. Use a flat-bladed knife to spread one-quarter of the reserved cream around the outside of the petits fours. Coat outside of the petits fours with the grated chocolate. Spoon cream on top of each petit four and top with a maraschino cherry. Serve chilled. (For image, see page 88.)

Nougatine and honey butter petits fours

Sponge

125 g (4½ oz/1 cup) plain (all-purpose) flour

2 teaspoons baking powder

55 g (2 oz/½ cup) ground almonds

125 g (4½ oz/½ cup) unsalted butter, softened

230 g (8¼ oz/1 cup) caster (superfine) sugar

4 eggs, separated

1 teaspoon natural vanilla extract

170 ml (5½ fl oz/⅔ cup) milk

Honey butter cream

100 g (3½ oz) unsalted butter, softened

40 g (1½ oz) honey

1 teaspoon natural vanilla extract

200 g (7 oz) icing (confectioners') sugar, sifted

Nougatine

65 g (2½ oz) sugar

65 ml (2¼ fl oz) liquid glucose

65 g (2½ oz) unsalted butter

65 g (2½ oz) chopped blanched almonds

makes
24

Preheat the oven to 180°C (350°F/Gas 4). Grease a 20 x 30 cm (8 x 12 inch) baking tin and line with baking paper. Line two baking trays with baking paper. Sift the flour, baking powder and ground almonds onto baking paper. Cream the butter and 145 g (5¼ oz/⅔ cup) sugar in a bowl using electric beaters until pale and fluffy. Beat in the egg yolks, then the vanilla. Fold in the flour mixture and milk until just combined. Beat the egg whites in a clean bowl until foamy. Add the remaining sugar and beat into soft peaks. Stir a tablespoonful of the egg white into the sponge mixture, then gently fold in the rest. Pour into the prepared tin. Bake for 25–30 minutes or until firm to the touch. Allow to cool in the tin for 5 minutes before turning out onto a rack to cool.

To make the butter cream, beat the butter, honey and vanilla until pale and creamy. Gradually add the sugar and beat until light and fluffy. For the nougatine, combine the sugar, glucose and butter in a frying pan over medium heat. Boil, until the sugar caramelises. Add almonds and shake the pan to coat. Pour onto the baking tray and cool. Transfer to a food processor and process until finely chopped.

Slice the sponge into three horizontal layers. Place one layer on the remaining prepared tray and spread with one-quarter of the butter cream. Top with another layer of sponge, then spread with another quarter of the butter cream. Top with the last layer of sponge, then freeze for 30 minutes or until firm. Using a 4 cm (1½ inch) heart-shaped cutter, cut out 24 shapes. Spread the sides of half the petits fours with half of the remaining butter cream. Spread the tops of the remaining petits fours with the remaining butter cream. Coat the sides and tops with nougatine. Serve chilled. (For image, see page 89.)

Portuguese tartlets

1 tablespoon sugar

2 x 25 cm (10 inch) square sheets ready-rolled puff
 pastry

plain (all-purpose) flour, for dusting

Custard

3 egg yolks

75 g (2½ oz/⅓ cup) sugar

½ tablespoon custard powder

100 ml (3½ fl oz) milk

80 ml (2½ fl oz/⅓ cup) cream

1 vanilla bean, split lengthways

makes
24

Preheat the oven to 200°C (400°F/Gas 6). Lightly grease two 12-hole mini muffin tins.

Sprinkle a 30 cm (12 inch) square work surface area with ½ tablespoon sugar. Place one pastry sheet on the sugar, cut in half and sit one half on top of the other. Repeat with the remaining pastry to give a double-layered sheet of pastry. Roll up each sheet of pastry from a short end to form two logs. Wrap each log in plastic wrap and chill in the refrigerator for 10 minutes.

Cut each log into 1 cm (½ inch) rounds. Lightly flour a work surface. Roll each pastry disc into a 10 cm (4 inch) round. Press rounds into muffin tins. Prick the bases well with a fork. Refrigerate until needed.

To make the custard, place the egg yolks, sugar and custard powder in a saucepan and whisk to combine. Gradually add the milk and cream, whisking until smooth. Add the vanilla bean, place over medium heat and cook, stirring constantly, until the mixture thickens and comes to the boil. Remove the vanilla bean and transfer the custard to a bowl. Cover the surface with plastic wrap (to prevent a skin from forming) and set aside to cool.

Divide the custard among the chilled pastry cases. Do not overfill or the custard will bubble over the pastry. Bake for 12–15 minutes, or until the custard is set and golden. Cool in the tins for 5 minutes before transferring to a wire rack to cool completely.

Mango and coconut napoleons

1 sheet ready-rolled puff pastry

60 g (2¼ oz/¼ cup) unsalted butter, melted

40 g (1½ oz/⅓ cup) icing (confectioners') sugar,
    plus extra, sifted, for dusting (optional)

1 ripe mango

125 ml (4 fl oz/½ cup) cream

1 teaspoon natural coconut extract

makes
12

Preheat the oven to 200°C (400°F/Gas 6). Line two baking trays with baking paper.

Use a 4 cm (1½ inch) heart-shaped cookie cutter to cut 24 hearts from the pastry. Place 12 hearts on each prepared tray. Prick the hearts on one tray all over with a fork to form the bases. Place in the freezer for 2 minutes. Cover each tray with a sheet of baking paper and top with another tray to flatten the pastry hearts. Bake for 4–5 minutes. Remove the top tray from the hearts that will form the lids and brush with the melted butter — this will allow them to rise. Bake the other tray for a further 2 minutes before removing the top tray and brushing the hearts with butter. Return trays to the oven. Cook 1–2 minutes, or until crisp and golden. Transfer to a wire rack to cool completely.

Preheat the grill (broiler) to medium–high. Dredge the hearts with 2 tablespoons of the icing sugar. Place on the unlined baking trays and place under the grill for 1–2 minutes, or until light golden and caramelised. Slice mango into 2–3 mm (¹⁄₁₆–⅛ inch) thick slices. Cut out 24 heart shapes.

Whisk the cream, the remaining icing sugar and the coconut extract until firm peaks form. Place a mango heart on each pastry base and spread on a thin layer of cream. Add another mango heart and a layer of cream and top with the lids. Dust with extra icing sugar, if desired, and serve immediately. Napoleons are best eaten on the day they are made.

Cranberry and fig mini puddings

four 3 cm (1¼ inch) thick slices white bread

5 egg yolks

100 g (3½ oz) caster (superfine) sugar

2 teaspoons finely grated orange zest

600 ml (21 fl oz) cream

1 vanilla bean, split lengthways and
    seeds scraped

60 g (2¼ oz/½ cup) sweetened dried cranberries
    (see NOTE page 59)

100 g (3½ oz) dried apricots, roughly chopped

100 g (3½ oz) dried figs, roughly chopped

icing (confectioners') sugar, sifted, for
    dusting (optional)

makes
24

Preheat the oven to 150°C (300°F/Gas 2). Grease and line a 20 x 30 cm (8 x 12 inch) baking tin with baking paper, extending the paper over the four sides for easy removal later.

Remove the crusts from the bread and cut into 3 cm (1¼ inch) cubes.

Beat the egg yolks and sugar in a small bowl with electric beaters until light and creamy. Add the zest and beat again briefly. Pour the cream into a saucepan and add the vanilla seeds. Bring to the boil and pour over the egg mixture, whisking constantly. Add the bread and toss to coat. Sprinkle half of the fruit into the prepared tin. Top with a layer of bread. Scatter with the remaining fruit and pour over the remaining egg mixture. Bake for 45–50 minutes, or until firm when tested with a skewer. Allow to cool completely in the tin. Transfer to the refrigerator and chill for at least 4 hours, or until firm.

Invert the pudding onto a cutting board or work surface and remove the paper. Use a 4 cm (1½ inch) cutter to cut out 24 rounds, or cut with a sharp serrated knife. (Cutting from the base is easier due to the bread becoming crisp on the top.) Dust with the icing sugar, if desired, and serve chilled.

Tangy lemon petits fours

450 g (1 lb) ready-made madeira cake

600 g (1 lb 5 oz/4 cups) white chocolate
   melts (buttons)

250 ml (9 fl oz/1 cup) cream

6 drops of rose pink food colouring

120 g (4¼ oz) raspberries

icing (confectioners') sugar, sifted, for dusting

Lemon curd

2 large egg yolks

55 g (2 oz/¼ cup) caster (superfine) sugar

½ tablespoon finely grated lemon zest

2½ tablespoons lemon juice

100 g (3½ oz) unsalted butter

makes
36

To make the lemon curd, beat the egg yolks and sugar in a heatproof bowl. Add the zest, juice and butter and place the bowl over a saucepan of barely simmering water (don't let the bowl touch the water). Stir over low heat for 10 minutes, or until the mixture thickens enough to coat the back of a wooden spoon. Cool slightly, then cover the surface with plastic wrap and leave until completely cold.

Trim the sides of the cake to make a 7.5 x 15 cm (3 x 6 inch) rectangle. Cut the cake horizontally into four slices. Spread two slices with the lemon curd and top each with another slice to form two cakes with two layers. Place in freezer for 20 minutes, or until firm. Cut each cake into 18, 2.5 cm (1 inch) squares. Place on a wire rack with a baking tray underneath.

Place half the white chocolate in a medium bowl. Bring the cream to the boil in a small saucepan over medium heat, pour over the chocolate and stir until smooth. Spoon the melted chocolate over the cakes until covered. Allow to sit for 5 minutes before transferring to a baking tray lined with baking paper. Refrigerate until needed.

Line another baking tray with baking paper. Place the remaining white chocolate in a heatproof bowl over a saucepan of simmering water — do not allow the bowl to touch the water. Add the food colouring and stir until smooth. Spread over the baking paper to a thickness of 1–2 mm (about 1/16 inch) and allow to set. Cut out squares to fit the outside of each petit four. Refrigerate until needed.

To serve, top each petit four with a raspberry and dust with the icing sugar.

Mini pavlovas

3 egg whites
125 g (4½ oz/1 cup) icing (confectioners') sugar
150 g (5½ oz) dark chocolate, melted
250 ml (9 fl oz/1 cup) thick
    (double/heavy) cream
1 tablespoon icing (confectioners') sugar, extra,
    sifted
1 teaspoon finely grated orange zest
assorted fresh fruit (such as strawberries, papaya
    and kiwi fruit), sliced, to serve
passionfruit pulp, to serve

makes
40

Preheat the oven to 150°C (300°F/Gas 2). Line two baking trays with baking paper. Use a 4 cm (1½ inch) cutter as a guide to draw 20 circles on each sheet of paper. Invert the paper on the trays (so the pencil won't come off on the pavlovas).

Place the egg whites in a large heatproof bowl and beat with electric beaters until stiff peaks form. Set bowl over a saucepan of simmering water, carefully add sugar and beat until mixture is thick and glossy.

Spread a little of the meringue mixture, following the marked rounds as a guide, over each sheet of baking paper—these will be the bases of the pavlovas. Spoon the remaining meringue mixture into a piping bag fitted with a 5 mm (¼ inch) plain piping (icing) nozzle. Pipe three small circles one on top of the other around the outer edge of each base to form a border. Bake for 30 minutes, or until firm to the touch. Cool in the oven with the door slightly ajar.

When completely cool, dip the base of each pavlova in melted chocolate to come about 2 mm (1⁄16 inch) up the side, then transfer to trays lined with baking paper and leave to set.

Place cream, extra icing sugar and orange zest in a bowl and stir to combine. If necessary, lightly beat until just thick. Spoon into a piping bag fitted with a small plain nozzle and pipe onto pavlovas. Top with the fruit and serve with the passionfruit pulp.

Meringue kisses with chocolate coffee cream

2 egg whites
¼ teaspoon almond essence
115 g (4 oz/½ cup) caster (superfine) sugar

Chocolate coffee cream
200 g (7 oz) dark chocolate, chopped
1 tablespoon instant coffee granules
125 ml (4 fl oz/½ cup) cream, for whipping

makes
20

Preheat the oven to 150°C (300°F/Gas 2). Line two baking trays with baking paper.

Place the egg whites in a large bowl and beat using electric beaters until firm peaks form. Mix in the almond essence, then add sugar, a spoonful at a time, and beat until the sugar has dissolved and mixture is thick and glossy. Transfer meringue mixture to a piping (icing) bag fitted with a 1 cm (½ inch) plain nozzle and pipe rounds at 3 cm (1¼ inch) intervals, allowing room for spreading, onto prepared trays. Or, place teaspoons of mixture, spacing them well apart, on the prepared trays. Bake for 45 minutes. Turn off the oven and leave the door slightly ajar, allowing the meringues to cool slowly.

To make the chocolate coffee cream, place the chocolate, coffee and cream in a heatproof bowl over a saucepan of simmering water, ensuring the bowl doesn't touch the water. Stir until the chocolate has melted and the mixture is smooth. Cool, cover with plastic wrap and refrigerate until required.

Use the chocolate coffee cream to sandwich the meringues together.

These filled meringues are best eaten immediately. Unfilled meringues will keep, stored in an airtight container, for up to 2 weeks.

Tiramisù hearts

two 14 x 20 cm (5½ x 8 inch) ready-made sponge
   cakes
1 tablespoon instant coffee powder
60 ml (2 fl oz/¼ cup) boiling water
2 tablespoons coffee liqueur
100 g (3½ oz) dark chocolate, chopped
2 tablespoons unsweetened cocoa powder

Filling
1 large egg
2 tablespoons icing (confectioners') sugar
1 teaspoon natural vanilla extract
150 g (5½ oz) mascarpone cheese
60 ml (2 fl oz/¼ cup) cream, whipped to soft peaks

makes
24

Grease and line the base and sides of a 20 x 30 cm
(8 x 12 inch) baking tin with baking paper. Line a
baking tray with baking paper.

Cut each cake horizontally into three 8 mm (⅜ inch)
layers. Combine the coffee, boiling water and liqueur
in a small bowl. Set aside to cool. Brush each of the
layers with the coffee mixture.

To make the filling, beat the egg, sugar and vanilla in
a bowl using electric beaters until pale and creamy.
Fold in the mascarpone and cream.

Place one layer of sponge in the prepared tin and
spread with one-third of the filling. Top with another
layer of sponge. Spread with another one-third of the
filling. Repeat with the remaining sponge and filling.
Place in the freezer for 40–50 minutes, or until firm.
Use a 4 cm (1½ inch) heart-shaped cutter to cut out
24 hearts.

Melt the chocolate in a heatproof bowl over a
saucepan of simmering water, ensuring the bowl
doesn't touch the water. Stir until the chocolate has
melted. Pour onto the prepared tray. Spread to a
thickness of 2 mm (1/16 inch) with a spatula. Allow to
set before cutting out 24 heart shapes with the
cutter used for the cakes.

Transfer the chocolate hearts to a wire rack and
dredge half with the cocoa. Place carefully on top of
the petits fours. Refrigerate until needed.

Cinnamon palmiers

Preheat the oven to 200°C (400°F/Gas 6). Line a large baking tray with baking paper.

Combine the sugar and cinnamon in a small bowl. Sprinkle half of the cinnamon sugar onto a clean work surface, place the pastry on top and sprinkle with the remaining cinnamon sugar. Gently roll over the pastry with a rolling pin to secure the sugar, brush with half the melted butter and slice in half. Use your fingers to gently roll up one long side as tightly as possible to the middle. Repeat with the remaining side and the remaining piece of pastry. Brush with remaining butter. Wrap the rolls tightly in plastic wrap. Freeze for 20 minutes, or until firm.

Use a small, sharp knife to cut across each roll into 1 cm (½ inch) thick slices. Place the palmiers, cut side up, 1–2 cm (½–¾ inch) apart, to allow for spreading, on the prepared tray. Bake for 8–10 minutes, or until beginning to caramelise. Remove the tray from the oven and carefully flip the palmiers over. Bake for a further 2–3 minutes. Transfer to a wire rack to cool, caramelised side up.

Store in an airtight container for up to 1 week.

55 g (2 oz/¼ cup) sugar

1 teaspoon ground cinnamon

1 x 25 cm (10 inch) square sheet ready-rolled
   puff pastry

30 g (1 oz) unsalted butter, melted

makes
50

Raspberry cream sponge petits fours

two 17 cm (6½ inch) square ready-made
   sponge cakes
150 ml (5 fl oz) cream
2 tablespoons icing (confectioners') sugar
250 g (9 oz/2 cups) raspberries

Jelly
80 g (2¾ oz) raspberries
2 tablespoons icing (confectioners') sugar
150 ml (5 fl oz) apple juice
2 teaspoons powdered gelatine
1 tablespoon Cointreau

makes
24

Spray a 24 cm (9½ inch) square baking tin with oil and line with plastic wrap, extending the plastic wrap over the four sides. Line a baking tray with foil.

To make the jelly, place the raspberries and sugar in the bowl of a food processor and process until smooth. Add 100 ml (3½ fl oz) of the apple juice and strain, discarding the seeds. Bring remaining apple juice to the boil, sprinkle over the gelatine and stir until the gelatine dissolves. Add gelatine mixture and the liqueur to the raspberry juice and stir well. Pour the jelly into the prepared tin. Refrigerate for 2–3 hours, or until set. Transfer to the freezer for 20 minutes.

Slice each cake horizontally into three 5 mm (¼ inch) thick layers. Use a 4 cm (1½ inch) flower cutter to cut out 48 discs. Turn the jelly out onto a work surface. Use the same cutter to cut out 24 flowers.

Whip the cream and sugar until soft peaks form. Spoon into a piping (icing) bag with a large star nozzle. Place 24 cake flowers on the prepared tray. Pipe a small amount of cream on each to secure the jelly. Top with a jelly flower and pipe on a small amount of cream. Place a sponge flower on top, pipe on more cream and decorate with a raspberry. Refrigerate until needed.

These are best eaten on the same day as assembling.

Lemon curd and blueberry tartlets

4 sheets ready-rolled shortcrust pastry

2 tablespoons icing (confectioners') sugar, sifted

48 blueberries

Lemon curd

150 ml (5 fl oz) lemon juice

2 teaspoons finely grated lemon zest

6 egg yolks

110 g (3¾ oz/½ cup) sugar

100 g (3½ oz) unsalted butter, cut into cubes

makes
48

To make the lemon curd, whisk the lemon juice and zest, egg yolks and sugar in a small saucepan. Place over low heat and cook for 2–3 minutes, or until the sugar has dissolved. Gradually add the butter, stirring constantly, and cook for 8–10 minutes, or until thick. Remove from the heat and cover the surface with plastic wrap to prevent a skin forming. Refrigerate until needed.

Preheat the oven to 180°C (350°F/Gas 4). Lightly grease 24, 3 cm (1¼ inch) tartlet tins. Line a baking tray with baking paper.

Cut 48 rounds from the pastry with a 5 cm (2 inch) cutter. Place half the rounds on the prepared baking tray, cover with plastic wrap and refrigerate until needed. Press the remaining pastry rounds into the prepared tins. Bake cases for 12–15 minutes, or until golden. Repeat with the remaining rounds. Allow to cool completely.

When cool, dust each tartlet case with icing sugar, spoon in 1 teaspoon of the lemon curd and top with a blueberry.

These tartlets are best eaten the day they are made. The cases can be baked up to 1 week in advance and stored in an airtight container. To revive them, heat in a 180°C (350°F/Gas 4) oven for 5 minutes. The curd can be made 2 days ahead. Assemble no more than 1 hour before serving.

Slices

Fig and cinnamon slice

125 g (4½ oz/½ cup) unsalted butter, softened

55 g (2 oz) soft brown sugar

1 teaspoon ground cinnamon

185 g (6½ oz/1½ cups) plain (all-purpose) flour, sifted

375 g (13 oz) dried figs

1 cinnamon stick

115 g (4 oz/½ cup) caster (superfine) sugar

375 ml (13 fl oz/1½ cups) boiling water

makes
15

Preheat the oven to 180°C (350°F/Gas 4). Lightly grease an 18 x 28 cm (7 x 11¼ inch) baking tin and line the base with baking paper, extending the paper over the long sides for easy removal later.

Beat the butter, brown sugar and ground cinnamon in a medium bowl with electric beaters until light and fluffy. Fold in the flour with a large metal spoon. Press the mixture evenly into the prepared tin and bake for 25 minutes. Cool slightly.

Combine the figs, cinnamon stick, caster sugar and water in a saucepan and bring to the boil. Reduce the heat and simmer for 20 minutes, or until the figs have softened and liquid has reduced by one-third. Remove the cinnamon stick and place the mixture in the bowl of a food processor. Process in short bursts until smooth. Pour onto the cooked base and bake for 10 minutes, or until set. Cool in the tin and when cold, lift out and cut into squares.

Lemon squares

125 g (4½ oz/½ cup) unsalted butter, softened
75 g (2½ oz) caster (superfine) sugar
155 g (5½ oz/1¼ cups) plain (all-purpose) flour, sifted
icing (confectioners') sugar, sifted, for dusting

Topping
4 eggs, lightly beaten
230 g (8¼ oz/1 cup) caster (superfine) sugar
60 ml (2 fl oz/¼ cup) lemon juice
1 teaspoon finely grated lemon zest
30 g (1 oz/¼ cup) plain (all-purpose) flour, sifted
½ teaspoon baking powder, sifted

makes
30

Preheat the oven to 180°C (350°F/Gas 4). Lightly grease a 20 x 30 cm (8 x 12 inch) baking tin and line the base with baking paper, extending the paper over two long sides for easy removal later.

Cream the butter and sugar in a medium bowl using electric beaters until pale and fluffy. Fold in the flour with a metal spoon. Press into the prepared tin and bake for 20 minutes, or until golden and firm. Set aside to cool.

To make the topping, beat the eggs and sugar in a large bowl with electric beaters for 2 minutes, or until pale and thick. Stir in the lemon juice and zest. Gradually add the flour and baking powder and whisk until combined. Pour onto the base and smooth the surface with a spatula. Bake for 25 minutes, or until just firm. Cool in the tin. Dust with the icing sugar, cut into pieces and serve.

Raspberry and coconut slice

280 g (10 oz/2¼ cups) plain (all-purpose) flour

3 tablespoons ground almonds

450 g (1 lb/2 cups) caster (superfine) sugar

250 g (9 oz/1 cup) unsalted butter, chilled and
 cut into cubes

½ teaspoon ground nutmeg

½ teaspoon baking powder

4 eggs

1 teaspoon natural vanilla extract

1 tablespoon lemon juice

300 g (10½ oz) fresh or thawed frozen raspberries

90 g (3¼ oz/1 cup) desiccated coconut

icing (confectioners') sugar, sifted, for dusting

makes
12

Preheat the oven to 180°C (350°F/Gas 4). Lightly grease a 20 x 30 cm (8 x 12 inch) baking tin and line the base with baking paper, extending the paper over two long sides for easy removal later.

Sift 220 g (7¾ oz/1¾ cups) of the flour into a large bowl. Add the almonds and 115 g (4 oz/½ cup) of the sugar and stir to combine. Rub in the butter with your fingertips until the mixture resembles fine breadcrumbs. Press into the prepared tin and then bake for 20–25 minutes, or until golden.

Reduce the oven temperature to 150°C (300°F/Gas 2). Sift nutmeg, baking powder and remaining flour onto a piece of baking paper. Beat the eggs, vanilla and remaining caster sugar in a large bowl with electric beaters for 4 minutes, or until light and creamy. Fold in the flour mixture with a large metal spoon. Stir in lemon juice, raspberries and coconut, then pour over the base. Bake for 1 hour, or until golden. You may need to cover with foil if the top browns too quickly. Set aside to cool in the tin, then cut into pieces. Dust with the icing sugar and serve.

Old English matrimonials

Preheat the oven to 180°C (350°F/Gas 4). Lightly grease a 16 x 26 cm (6¼ x 10½ inch) baking tin and line the base with baking paper, extending the paper over the long sides for easy removal later.

Combine the oats, flour, sugar, butter, salt, coconut and a pinch of salt in a large bowl. Press half the oat mixture into the prepared tin. Spread the jam on top. Sprinkle over the remaining oat mixture and press lightly with your fingertips to flatten.

Bake on the lowest shelf in the oven for 15 minutes, then transfer to the middle shelf to bake for a further 15 minutes, or until the top is golden brown. Allow to cool in the tin, then slice into pieces and serve.

200 g (7 oz/2 cups) quick-cooking rolled (porridge) oats
220 g (7¾ oz/1¾ cups) plain (all-purpose) flour
230 g (8¼ oz/1¼ cups) soft brown sugar
250 g (9 oz/1 cup) unsalted butter, melted
90 g (3¼ oz/1 cup) desiccated coconut
315 g (11 oz/1 cup) strawberry jam, slightly warmed

makes
15

Sugar and spice slice

4 eggs

125 g (4½ oz/1 cup) icing (confectioners') sugar

¼ teaspoon ground cloves

¼ teaspoon ground cardamom

¼ teaspoon freshly grated nutmeg

2 teaspoons ground cinnamon

1 teaspoon finely grated lemon zest

150 g (5½ oz/1½ cups) ground almonds

100 g (3½ oz) ground hazelnuts

185 g (6½ oz/1 cup) mixed peel (mixed candied
    citrus peel)

Icing

250 g (9 oz/2 cups) icing (confectioners') sugar

1 tablespoon butter, softened

2 tablespoons dark rum

1 tablespoon hot water

30 blanched almonds, to decorate

makes
15

Preheat the oven to 200°C (400°F/Gas 6). Lightly grease a 16 x 26 cm (6¼ x 10½ inch) baking tin and line the base with baking paper, extending the paper over the long sides for easy removal later.

Place the eggs and sugar in a bowl and beat with electric beaters for 5 minutes, or until frothy. Fold in the spices, lemon zest, almonds, hazelnuts, mixed peel and a pinch of salt. Pour into the tin and bake for 25 minutes, or until lightly golden. Remove from the oven and cool in the tin for 15 minutes, then lift onto a wire rack to cool completely.

To make the icing, sift the sugar into a large bowl and stir in the butter. Add the rum and water and mix until combined.

Cut the slice into pieces. Use a spatula to spread the icing over each piece and decorate the top with two almonds. Allow the icing to set before serving.

Peach and sour cream slice

150 g (5½ oz) unsalted butter, softened

115 g (4 oz/½ cup) caster (superfine) sugar

1 teaspoon natural vanilla extract

3 eggs

155 g (5½ oz/1¼ cups) self-raising flour, sifted

125 ml (4 fl oz/½ cup) milk

45 g (1⅔ oz/½ cup) desiccated coconut

½ teaspoon ground cardamom

300 g (10½ oz) sour cream

6 peaches, peeled and sliced or 2 x 410 g (14½ oz)
   tins peach slices, drained and patted dry

75 g (2½ oz/⅓ cup) raw (demerara) sugar

makes
15

Preheat the oven to 170°C (325°F/Gas 3). Lightly grease a 16 x 26 cm (6¼ x 10½ inch) baking tin and line the base with baking paper, extending the paper over the long sides for easy removal later.

Cream the butter, caster sugar and vanilla in a large bowl using electric beaters until pale and fluffy. Add two of the eggs, one at a time, beating well after each addition. Fold in the flour and milk, in batches, alternating between the two. Fold in the coconut and cardamom. Use a spatula to spread the mixture into the prepared tin. Bake for 20 minutes, or until a skewer inserted in the centre comes out clean. Allow to cool slightly.

Meanwhile, increase the oven temperature to 200°C (400°F/Gas 6). Mix the sour cream and the remaining egg in a small bowl and spread over the cooked base. Arrange the peaches over the filling. Sprinkle with the raw sugar and bake for 30–40 minutes, or until golden and set on top. Allow to cool in the tin before slicing into fingers.

Nanaimo bars

200 g (7 oz) digestive biscuits (cookies)

80 g (2¾ oz) pecans

40 g (1½ oz/⅓ cup) unsweetened cocoa powder

90 g (3¼ oz/1 cup) desiccated coconut

125 g (4½ oz/½ cup) unsalted butter, melted

Filling

60 g (2¼ oz/¼ cup) unsalted butter, softened

2 tablespoons custard powder

1 teaspoon natural vanilla extract

60 ml (2 fl oz/¼ cup) milk

250 g (9 oz/2 cups) icing (confectioners') sugar

Topping

200 g (7 oz) dark chocolate, chopped

2 teaspoons vegetable oil

makes
15

Lightly grease a 16 x 26 cm (6¼ x 10½ inch) baking tin and line the base with baking paper, extending the paper over the long sides for easy removal later.

Place the biscuits, pecans, cocoa and coconut in the bowl of a food processor and process until ground. Add the butter and pulse in short bursts until well combined. Press into the prepared tin. Refrigerate for 20 minutes.

To make the filling, place the butter, custard powder, vanilla, milk and sugar in the clean bowl of the food processor. Process until thick and creamy, then spread over the base.

To make the topping, place the chocolate and oil in a heatproof bowl. Half-fill a saucepan with water, bring to the boil and remove from the heat. Place the bowl over the saucepan, making sure the base doesn't touch the water. Stir occasionally, until the chocolate has melted. Use a spatula to spread the topping over the filling. Refrigerate until the chocolate has set. Cut into pieces.

Classic brownies

125 g (4½ oz) dark chocolate, chopped

90 g (3¼ oz/⅓ cup) unsalted butter, softened

230 g (8¼ oz/1 cup) caster (superfine) sugar

1 teaspoon natural vanilla extract

2 eggs

85 g (3 oz/⅔ cup) plain (all-purpose) flour, sifted

30 g (1 oz/¼ cup) unsweetened cocoa powder, sifted

½ teaspoon baking powder, sifted

icing (confectioners') sugar, for dusting

makes
16

Preheat the oven to 180°C (350°F/Gas 4). Grease a 17 cm (6½ inch) square baking tin and line the base with baking paper, extending the paper over two opposite sides for easy removal later.

Place the chocolate in a heatproof bowl. Half-fill a saucepan with water, bring to the boil and remove from the heat. Place the bowl over the saucepan, ensuring the base of the bowl doesn't touch the water. Stir occasionally until chocolate has melted. Cool slightly.

Cream the butter, sugar and vanilla in a medium bowl with electric beaters until pale and fluffy. Add the eggs, one at a time, beating well after each addition. Stir in the chocolate.

Fold in the combined flour, cocoa and baking powder with a metal spoon. Pour into the prepared tin and smooth the surface with a spatula. Bake for 30–35 minutes, or until firm to touch and the sides come away from the tin easily. Cool in tin. Remove, cut into squares and serve, dusted with icing sugar.

Ginger shortbread slice

220 g (7¾ oz) unsalted butter, softened

115 g (4 oz/½ cup) caster (superfine) sugar

280 g (10 oz/2¼ cups) plain (all-purpose) flour

45 g (1⅔ oz/¼ cup) rice flour

1 tablespoon ground ginger

Topping

185 g (6½ oz/1½ cups) icing (confectioners') sugar

60 g (2¼ oz/¼ cup) unsalted butter

90 g (3¼ oz/¼ cup) golden syrup (light treacle)

2 teaspoons ground ginger

100 g (3½ oz) glacé (candied) ginger,
   finely chopped

makes
15

Preheat the oven to 180°C (350°F/Gas 4). Lightly grease a 16 x 26 cm (6¼ x 10½ inch) baking tin and line the base and sides with baking paper, extending the paper over the long sides for easy removal later.

Cream the butter and sugar in a bowl with electric beaters until pale and fluffy. Sift the flours, ginger and a pinch of salt onto a sheet of baking paper, then fold into the butter mixture until well combined. Use a spatula to smooth the mixture into the prepared tin. Bake for 20–25 minutes, or until light golden brown. Cool slightly.

To make the topping, place the sugar, butter, golden syrup and ground ginger in a saucepan over low heat. Stir until the butter has melted and the mixture is smooth. Pour over the warm base and sprinkle with the glacé ginger. Allow to cool in the tin before cutting into pieces.

Jam and ricotta streusel

125 g (4½ oz/1 cup) plain (all-purpose) flour

½ teaspoon baking powder

45 g (1²/₃ oz/¼ cup) soft brown sugar

55 g (2 oz/½ cup) ground almonds

150 g (5½ oz) unsalted butter, chilled and
     cut into cubes

1 teaspoon natural vanilla extract

1 egg

315 g (11 oz/1 cup) apricot or jam of choice,
     slightly warmed

Filling

650 g (1 lb 7 oz) ricotta cheese

80 g (2¾ oz/⅓ cup) caster (superfine) sugar

80 g (2¾ oz/½ cup) pine nuts, lightly toasted

2 tablespoons dark rum

2 eggs, lightly beaten

makes
15

Lightly grease a 16 x 26 cm (6¼ x 10½ inch) baking tin and line the base with baking paper, extending the paper over the long sides for easy removal later.

Place the flour, baking powder, brown sugar, ground almonds and a pinch of salt in the bowl of a food processor. Process until combined. Add the butter and pulse in short bursts until the mixture resembles breadcrumbs. Add the vanilla and egg and pulse until the mixture just comes together. Press half of the dough into the prepared tin and refrigerate for 30 minutes. Wrap the remaining dough in plastic wrap and refrigerate until required.

Preheat the oven to 180°C (350°F/Gas 4).

Meanwhile, to make the filling, put the ricotta, sugar, pine nuts, rum and egg in a large bowl and mix well to combine.

Spread the warm jam over the base and cover with the ricotta filling. Crumble the remaining dough over the filling and bake for 40 minutes, or until golden. Allow to cool completely in the tin before cutting into fingers and serving.

Rocky road slice

400 g (14 oz) white chocolate, chopped

250 g (9 oz/2¾ cups) pink and white
   marshmallows, chopped

150 g (5½ oz) dried strawberries or Turkish delight,
   roughly chopped

45 g (1⅔ oz/¾ cup) shredded coconut, toasted

100 g (3½ oz) shortbread biscuits (cookies),
   roughly chopped

400 g (14 oz) milk chocolate, chopped

makes
15

Lightly grease a 16 x 26 cm (6¼ x 10½ inch) baking
tin and line the base with baking paper, extending the
paper over the long sides for easy removal later.

Place the white chocolate in a heatproof bowl.
Half-fill a saucepan with water, bring to the boil and
remove from the heat. Sit bowl over the saucepan,
making sure the base of the bowl doesn't touch the
water. Stir occasionally until chocolate has melted.
Cool slightly. Pour into the tin.

Sprinkle the marshmallow pieces, strawberries
or Turkish delight, coconut and biscuit pieces over
the chocolate base.

Melt the milk chocolate in a heatproof bowl over a
saucepan of just-boiled water, making sure the base
of the bowl doesn't touch the water. Cool slightly.
Pour over the base and filling, then refrigerate until
set. Cut into squares and serve.

Snickerdoodle slice

2 eggs

250 ml (9 fl oz/1 cup) milk

250 g (9 oz/2 cups) plain (all-purpose) flour

230 g (8¼ oz/1 cup) caster (superfine) sugar

1 tablespoon ground cinnamon

2 teaspoons baking powder

125 g (4½ oz/½ cup) unsalted butter, melted

thick (double/heavy) cream, to serve (optional)

Cinnamon sugar

3 tablespoons sugar

3 teaspoons ground cinnamon

makes
20

Preheat the oven to 180°C (350°F/Gas 4). Lightly grease a 20 x 30 cm (8 x 12 inch) baking tin and line the base with baking paper, extending the paper over two long sides for easy removal later.

Place the eggs and milk in a small bowl and whisk to combine. Sift the flour, sugar, cinnamon and baking powder into a large bowl. Make a well in the centre, pour in the egg mixture and stir with a metal spoon to roughly combine. Fold in the butter until smooth—do not overmix. Spoon half the dough into the prepared tin and smooth the surface with a spatula.

To make the cinnamon sugar, combine the sugar and cinnamon in a small bowl and mix well.

Sprinkle two-thirds of the cinnamon sugar over the dough in the tin. Gently spoon the remaining dough over the top and smooth the surface. Dust with the remaining cinnamon sugar. Bake for 25–30 minutes, or until firm. Cool in the tin for 20 minutes, then lift onto a wire rack to cool completely. Cut into pieces and serve with the cream, if desired.

Choc mallow bars

155 g (5½ oz/1¼ cups) plain (all-purpose) flour

30 g (1 oz/¼ cup) icing (confectioners') sugar

150 g (5½ oz) unsalted butter, melted

1 egg

160 g (5¾ oz/½ cup) raspberry jam, slightly
   warmed

250 g (9 oz/2¾ cups) white marshmallows

80 ml (2½ fl oz/⅓ cup) cream

160 g (5¾ oz/1 cup) chopped unsalted peanuts

200 g (7 oz) milk chocolate, chopped

2 teaspoons vegetable oil

makes
15

Preheat the oven to 200°C (400°F/Gas 6). Lightly grease a 16 x 26 cm (6¼ x 10½ inch) baking tin and line the base with baking paper, extending the paper over the long sides for easy removal later.

Sift the flour, sugar and a pinch of salt into a large bowl. Add the butter and the egg, and mix well to combine. Press the dough into the prepared tin and refrigerate for 20 minutes. Transfer to the oven to bake for 20 minutes. Remove from the oven and allow to cool. Spread the jam over the base.

Place marshmallows and cream in a saucepan. Stir over low heat for 5 minutes, or until marshmallows have melted. Pour over the base. Sprinkle the peanuts over the top.

Place the chocolate in a heatproof bowl. Half-fill a saucepan with water, bring to the boil and remove from the heat. Place bowl over the saucepan, ensuring the base of the bowl doesn't touch the water. Stand, stirring occasionally, until the chocolate has melted. Stir in the oil and cool slightly. Pour the chocolate evenly over the top of the slice and refrigerate until set. Cut into fingers and serve.

Quince linzer slice

Preheat the oven to 180°C (350°F/Gas 4). Lightly grease a 20 cm (8 inch) square baking tin and line the base with baking paper, extending the paper over two opposite sides for easy removal later.

Sift flour into a large bowl. Rub the butter cubes into the flour with your fingertips until mixture resembles fine breadcrumbs. Stir in the sugar, ground almonds and cinnamon. Make a well in the centre and add the egg yolk, lemon zest and juice. Mix with a flat-bladed knife, using a cutting action, until the mixture comes together in beads. Gather together and place on a lightly floured work surface. Shape into a ball, flatten slightly, wrap in plastic wrap and chill in the refrigerator for at least 1 hour.

Lightly flour a work surface and roll out two-thirds of the pastry to fit the base of the prepared tin. Press into the tin and refrigerate for 30 minutes. Prick the base all over with a fork, then spread on the jam.

Cut the remaining dough into strips and arrange over the jam in a lattice pattern. Bake for 35–40 minutes, or until the pastry is golden brown. Set aside to cool slightly, then dust with the icing sugar, if desired, while still warm. Cut into pieces and serve.

110 g (3¾ oz) plain (all-purpose) flour
110 g (3¾ oz) unsalted butter, chilled and cut into cubes
55 g (2 oz/¼ cup) caster (superfine) sugar
100 g (3½ oz/1 cup) ground almonds
¼ teaspoon ground cinnamon
1 egg yolk, lightly beaten
2 teaspoons finely grated lemon zest
1 tablespoon lemon juice
200 g (7 oz) quince jam, slightly warmed
icing (confectioners') sugar, sifted, for dusting (optional)

makes
16

Ginger cheesecake slice

200 g (7 oz) ginger-flavoured biscuits (cookies),
  finely crushed

60 g (2¼ oz/¼ cup) unsalted butter, melted

½ teaspoon ground cinnamon

500 g (1 lb 2 oz/2 cups) cream cheese, at room
  temperature

175 g (6 oz/½ cup) golden syrup (light treacle)

2 tablespoons caster (superfine) sugar

2 eggs, lightly beaten

55 g (2 oz/¼ cup) finely chopped crystallised ginger

125 ml (4 fl oz/½ cup) cream, lightly whipped

Topping

125 ml (4 fl oz/½ cup) cream

2 teaspoons caster (superfine) sugar

55 g (2 oz/¼ cup) thinly sliced crystallised ginger

makes
24

Preheat the oven to 170°C (325°F/Gas 3). Lightly grease a 20 x 30 cm (8 x 12 inch) baking tin and line the base with baking paper, extending the paper over two long sides for easy removal later.

Combine the biscuits, butter and cinnamon in a bowl and mix well. Press into the prepared tin. Refrigerate for 30 minutes, or until firm.

Beat the cream cheese, golden syrup and sugar in a medium bowl using electric beaters until light and fluffy. Add the eggs, one at a time, beating well after each addition. Fold in the ginger and whipped cream. Spread over the base and bake for 25 minutes, or until it is just set. Turn off the oven, leave the door slightly ajar and cool in the oven. Remove from the tin when completely cool and trim the edges.

To make the topping, beat the cream and caster sugar in a large bowl using electric beaters until soft peaks form.

Spread topping over the trimmed cheesecake using a spatula. Use a hot dry knife to cut the cheesecake into three strips lengthways and then cut each strip into eight pieces. Decorate with the ginger and serve.

Cardamom and almond barfi

Lightly grease a 16 x 26 cm (6¼ x 10½ inch) baking tin and line the base with baking paper, extending the paper over the long sides for easy removal later.

Place the almonds in the bowl of a food processor and process until ground. Transfer to a large bowl. Add the powdered milk, cardamom and butter and mix until well combined.

Combine the sugar and water in a small saucepan and stir over low heat until the sugar has dissolved. Allow to simmer, without stirring, for 5 minutes, or until reduced and syrupy. Quickly pour onto the almond mixture and stir well. Transfer to the tin, smooth the surface with a spatula and scatter over the gold leaf or cachous, if using. Refrigerate until firm. Cut into pieces and serve.

450 g (1 lb) blanched almonds, toasted

150 g (5½ oz/1½ cups) powdered milk

½ teaspoon ground cardamom

50 g (1¾ oz) butter, cut into cubes

230 g (8¼ oz/1 cup) caster (superfine) sugar

250 ml (9 fl oz/1 cup) water

gold leaf or cachous (optional)

makes
15

Choc chip pecan slice

185 g (6½ oz/1½ cups) self-raising flour

95 g (3¼ oz/½ cup) soft brown sugar

125 g (4½ oz/½ cup) unsalted butter, melted and slightly cooled

170 g (6 oz/1 cup) chocolate chips

Topping

3 eggs, at room temperature, lightly beaten

125 g (4½ oz/⅔ cup) soft brown sugar

50 g (1¾ oz) butter, melted

175 g (6 oz/½ cup) golden syrup (light treacle)

1 teaspoon natural vanilla extract

200 g (7 oz/2 cups) pecans

makes
15

Preheat the oven to 180°C (350°F/Gas 4). Lightly grease a 16 x 26 cm (6¼ x 10½ inch) baking tin and line the base with baking paper, extending the paper over the long sides for easy removal later.

Sift the flour into a large bowl. Add sugar and mix to combine. Add the butter, mix well and fold in the chocolate chips. Press into the tin and refrigerate for 20 minutes. Transfer to the oven and then bake for 20 minutes, or until lightly browned. Remove from the oven and allow to cool.

To make the topping, combine the eggs, sugar, butter, golden syrup and vanilla extract in a bowl, mixing well. Roughly chop half the pecans and stir into the mixture.

Pour topping over the cooled base and scatter on the remaining pecans. Bake for 30–40 minutes, or until the topping has set. Cover with foil if the nuts are browning too quickly. Allow to cool in the tin before slicing into pieces and serving.

Rose cheesecake slice

250 g (9 oz) plain sweet biscuits (cookies)

150 g (5½ oz) unsalted butter, melted

100 g (3½ oz) white chocolate, chopped

125 g (4½ oz/½ cup) cream cheese, at
    room temperature

2 tablespoons caster (superfine) sugar

90 g (3¼ oz/⅓ cup) sour cream

2 tablespoons boiling water

2 teaspoons powdered gelatine

150 ml (5 fl oz) cream, lightly whipped

Rose jelly

220 g (7¾ oz/1 cup) sugar

250 ml (9 fl oz/1 cup) water

400 ml (14 fl oz) pink Champagne

2 drops of rosewater

1½ tablespoons powdered gelatine

15 edible rose petals (optional)

makes
15

Preheat oven to 170°C (325°F/Gas 3). Grease a 16 x
26 cm (6¼ x 10½ inch) baking tin. Line the base with
baking paper, extending the paper over the long sides.

Place biscuits in the bowl of a food processor. Process
until ground. Add the butter and pulse in short bursts
until combined. Press mixture into tin. Refrigerate for
20 minutes. Bake for 15 minutes, until golden. Cool.

Place chocolate in a heatproof bowl. Half-fill a pan
with water, bring to the boil and remove from heat.
Sit bowl over the pan, ensuring it doesn't touch the
water. Stir occasionally, until melted. Cool slightly.

Place the cream cheese, sugar and sour cream in a
bowl and beat with electric beaters until well
combined and smooth.

Pour the boiling water into a small, heatproof bowl.
Add the gelatine and stir until dissolved completely.
Stir into the melted chocolate. Fold in the whipped
cream and cream cheese mixture, spoon over the
base and place in the refrigerator until set.

To make the rose jelly, place the sugar and water in a
saucepan. Cook, stirring, over low heat until the sugar
dissolves. Simmer, without stirring, for 5 minutes,
or until reduced and syrupy. Stir in Champagne and
rosewater, sprinkle over the gelatine and whisk to
combine. Pour into a bowl, refrigerate for 2 hours,
or until nearly set. Carefully spoon rose jelly over
filling, smoothing the surface. Refrigerate until set.
Cut into squares. Decorate with rose petals.

Key lime slice

100 g (3½ oz) plain (all-purpose) flour

50 g (1¾ oz) icing (confectioners') sugar

75 g (2½ oz) unsalted butter, chilled and cut
   into cubes

icing (confectioners') sugar, sifted, for dusting

raspberries, to serve (optional)

Lime topping

4 eggs

400 g (14 oz) tin condensed milk

150 ml (5 fl oz) lime juice

1 tablespoon finely grated lime zest

50 g (1¾ oz) plain (all-purpose) flour

makes
12

Preheat the oven to 180°C (350°F/Gas 4). Lightly grease an 18 x 28 cm (7 x 10¾ inch) baking tin and line the base with baking paper, extending the paper over the long sides for easy removal later.

Place flour, sugar and butter in the bowl of a food processor and pulse in short bursts until fine and crumbly. Press into tin and bake for 12–15 minutes, or until pale golden. Remove from the oven and set aside to cool slightly. Reduce the oven temperature to 150°C (300°F/Gas 2).

To make the lime topping, whisk the eggs and condensed milk in a medium bowl, then stir in the lime juice and zest. Sift in the flour and mix well.

Pour the lime topping over the base and bake for 30–40 minutes, or until firm. Set aside to completely cool in the tin, then cut into fingers and dust with the icing sugar. Serve with raspberries, if desired.

Truffle macaroon slice

3 egg whites

170 g (6 oz/¾ cup) caster (superfine) sugar

180 g (6¼ oz/2 cups) desiccated coconut

250 g (9 oz) dark chocolate, chopped

300 ml (10½ fl oz) cream

1 tablespoon unsweetened cocoa powder, sifted,
   for dusting

makes
24

Preheat the oven to 180°C (350°F/Gas 4). Lightly grease a 20 x 30 cm (8 x 12 inch) baking tin and line the base with baking paper, extending the paper over two long sides for easy removal later.

Beat the egg whites in a large bowl until soft peaks form. Gradually add the sugar, beating well after each addition until stiff and glossy. Fold in the coconut. Spread into the prepared tin and bake for 20 minutes, or until pale golden brown. While still warm, lightly but firmly press down into the tin with a spatula. Cool completely.

Place the chocolate in a heatproof bowl. Half-fill a saucepan with water, bring to the boil, then remove from the heat. Place the bowl over the saucepan, making sure the base of the bowl doesn't touch the water. Stand, stirring occasionally, until the chocolate has melted. Cool slightly.

Beat the cream until soft peaks form. Gently fold in the melted chocolate until well combined—do not overmix or it will curdle. Spread over the macaroon base and refrigerate for 3 hours, or until set. Remove from the tin, dust with the cocoa and cut into fingers.

Hazelnut meringue and chocolate layer slice

100 g (3½ oz/¾ cup) hazelnuts, lightly toasted
   and skinned
30 g (1 oz/¼ cup) cornflour (cornstarch)
40 g (1½ oz/⅓ cup) icing (confectioners') sugar
5 egg whites
200 g (7 oz) caster (superfine) sugar
unsweetened cocoa powder, sifted, for dusting

Ganache
250 g (9 oz) dark chocolate, chopped
125 ml (4 fl oz/½ cup) cream
2 tablespoons Frangelico

makes
18

Preheat the oven to 170°C (325°F/Gas 3). Lightly grease two 26 x 38 cm (10½ x 15 inch) baking trays and line with baking paper.

Place the hazelnuts, cornflour and icing sugar in the bowl of a food processor and process in short bursts until the mixture resembles coarse breadcrumbs.

Beat the egg whites in a large bowl using electric beaters until soft peaks form. Gradually add the caster sugar and beat until thick and glossy. Lightly fold the egg whites into the hazelnut mixture.

Divide the mixture evenly between the two trays and smooth the surface with a spatula. Bake for 30 minutes, or until light golden.

Trim the edges and cut a 26 cm (10½ inch) square from each meringue, reserving the trimmings. Allow to cool completely.

To make the ganache, place the chocolate, cram and Frangelico in a heatproof bowl. Half-fill a saucepan with water, bring to the boil and remove from the heat. Sit the bowl over the pan, making sure it does not touch the water. Stir occasionally, until the chocolate has just melted. Leave to cool completely, stirring occasionally.

Line a 26 cm (10½ inch) square baking tin with baking paper, extending the paper over two opposite sides. Line the base with one meringue square and carefully spread on half the ganache. Place the reserved meringue trimmings side by side over the ganache, then smooth the remaining ganache over the top. Finish with the remaining meringue square, press down gently and refrigerate for 1 hour. Remove the slice from the refrigerator. Dust with cocoa and cut into thin fingers with a serrated knife.

NOTES Toast the hazelnuts in a 180°C (350°F/Gas 4) oven for 5–10 minutes, or until lightly golden. Tip the nuts onto a clean tea towel (dish towel) and rub gently to remove the skins.

Chestnut cream slice

Chocolate sponges

80 g (2¾ oz) self-raising flour

60 g (2¼ oz/½ cup) plain (all-purpose) flour

1 tablespoon unsweetened cocoa powder

110 g (3¾ oz) caster (superfine) sugar

2 eggs, lightly beaten

2 teaspoons natural vanilla extract

120 g (4¼ oz/½ cup) unsalted butter, softened

125 ml (4 fl oz/½ cup) milk

125 ml (4 fl oz/½ cup) brandy

Base

60 g (2¼ oz/½ cup) plain (all-purpose) flour

2 tablespoons unsweetened cocoa powder

2 tablespoons caster (superfine) sugar

60 g (2¼ oz/¼ cup) unsalted butter, melted

1 tablespoon milk

½ teaspoon natural vanilla extract

makes
16

Preheat the oven to 180°C (350°F/Gas 4). Grease two 17 cm (6½ inch) square baking tins and line the bases and sides with baking paper.

To make the chocolate sponges, sift the flours and the cocoa into a large bowl, stir in the sugar and make a well in the centre. Combine the egg, vanilla extract, butter and milk in a separate bowl, pour into the well and stir until just combined. Divide evenly between the prepared tins and bake for 10–15 minutes, or until the top springs back on each cake when lightly touched. Set aside to cool for 5 minutes, then turn out onto wire racks to cool completely. Brush the top of each cake with the brandy.

Increase the oven temperature to 190°C (375°F/ Gas 5). Lightly grease a 17 cm (6½ inch) square baking tin. Line the base with baking paper, extending the paper over two opposite sides for easy removal later.

To make the base, sift the flour, cocoa and sugar into a bowl. Add the butter, milk and vanilla and mix until well combined. Press into the prepared tin and then smooth the top with the back of a spoon. Refrigerate for 20 minutes. Cover the dough with baking paper, fill with baking beads or uncooked rice and bake for 10–15 minutes, or until dry. Remove the paper and weights. Reduce the oven temperature to 180°C (350°F/Gas 4) and bake for 8–10 minutes, or until deep brown. Leave to cool.

To make the chestnut cream, beat the butter, chestnut purée, sugar and brandy in a bowl using electric beaters until smooth.

Spread half the chestnut cream over the cooled base and place one layer of chocolate sponge on the top, pressing down gently. Repeat with the remaining chestnut cream and chocolate sponge.

To make the chocolate glaze, place the chocolate, butter and cream in a heatproof bowl. Half-fill a saucepan with water, bring to the boil and remove from the heat. Place the bowl over the saucepan, making sure the base of the bowl doesn't touch the water. Stir occasionally until the chocolate and butter have melted. Stir until smooth and well combined. Set aside to cool.

Spread the chocolate glaze over the slice and leave to set. Cut into pieces and serve. (For image, see page 137.)

Chestnut cream
30 g (1 oz) unsalted butter, softened
250 g (9 oz/1 cup) unsweetened chestnut purée
60 g (2 oz/½ cup) icing (confectioner's) sugar
2 tablespoons brandy

Chocolate glaze
100 g (3 ½ oz) dark chocolate, chopped
60 g (2 oz/ ¼ cup) unsalted butter, chopped
1 tablespoon cream

Cider crumble slice

20 g (¾ oz) unsalted butter

1½ tablespoons golden syrup (light treacle)

150 ml (5 fl oz) alcoholic apple cider

250 g (9 oz/2 cups) self-raising flour

pinch of ground ginger

45 g (1⅔ oz/¼ cup) soft brown sugar

75 g (2½ oz) pitted dates, chopped

75 g (2½ oz/¾ cup) walnut halves, chopped

1 egg

Topping

1 large granny smith apple

40 g (1½ oz) unsalted butter

2½ tablespoons caster (superfine) sugar

60 g (2¼ oz/½ cup) plain (all-purpose) flour

75 g (2½ oz/¾ cup) walnut halves, chopped

makes
24

Preheat the oven to 170°C (325°F/Gas 3). Lightly grease a 20 x 30 cm (8 x 12 inch) baking tin and line the base with baking paper, extending the paper over two long sides for easy removal later.

Melt the butter and golden syrup in a saucepan over low heat. Remove from the heat and stir in the cider.

Sift the flour and ginger into a medium bowl. Stir in the sugar, dates and walnuts. Add the golden syrup mixture and the egg and beat until smooth. Spoon into the prepared tin and smooth the surface with a spatula.

To make the topping, peel, core and thinly slice the apple, then cut into 1.5 cm (⅝ inch) pieces. Melt the butter in a small saucepan, add the sugar, flour, apple and walnuts, stirring well. Spread over the base. Bake for 30 minutes, or until golden and a skewer inserted in the centre comes out clean. Cool in the tin. Cut into pieces and serve.

Choc honeycomb slice

Lightly grease a 16 x 26 cm (6¼ x 10½ inch) baking tin and line the base and sides with baking paper, extending the paper over the long sides for easy removal later.

Place the butter, chocolate and golden syrup in a saucepan. Cook, stirring occasionally, over low heat for 5 minutes, or until the chocolate has melted. Stir through the biscuits and honeycomb. Pour into the prepared tin and use a spatula to smooth the top. Refrigerate until set. Cut into pieces and serve.

100 g (3½ oz) unsalted butter, roughly chopped

300 g (10½ oz) milk chocolate, roughly chopped

115 g (4 oz/⅓ cup) golden syrup (light treacle)

200 g (7 oz) digestive biscuits (cookies), roughly broken up

100 g (3½ oz) honeycomb, roughly broken up

makes
18

Macadamia fingers

180 g (6¼ oz) unsalted butter, softened

1 teaspoon natural vanilla extract

80 g (2¾ oz/⅓ cup) caster (superfine) sugar

250 g (9 oz/2 cups) plain (all-purpose) flour, sifted

Topping

125 g (4½ oz/½ cup) unsalted butter

2 x 400 g (14 oz) tins condensed milk

2 tablespoons golden syrup (light treacle)

200 g (7 oz/1¼ cups) macadamia nuts,
   coarsely chopped

makes
18

Preheat the oven to 180°C (350°F/Gas 4). Lightly grease a 20 x 30 cm (8 x 12 inch) baking tin and line the base and sides with baking paper, extending the paper over the long sides for easy removal later.

Place the butter, vanilla and sugar in a large bowl and cream with electric beaters until pale and fluffy. Stir in the flour and mix until well combined. Press the mixture firmly into the prepared tin and bake for 25 minutes, or until the base is cooked and a little browned. Cool slightly.

To make the topping, place the butter, condensed milk and golden syrup in a saucepan and stir over low heat until the butter has melted. Increase the heat to medium and stir constantly for 15–20 minutes, or until the mixture is thick and caramel-like. Add the macadamias and pour onto the biscuit base. Bake for 10 minutes, or until golden. Cool in the tin. Remove from the tin, cut in half lengthways, then cut into fingers and serve.

Semolina syrup slice

300 g (10½ oz/2½ cups) coarse semolina

1 teaspoon bicarbonate of soda (baking soda)

250 ml (9 fl oz/1 cup) milk

250 g (9 oz/1 cup) plain yoghurt

125 g (4½ oz/½ cup) unsalted butter, melted

2 tablespoons honey

16 blanched almonds

460 g (1 lb ¼ oz/2 cups) caster (superfine) sugar

500 ml (17 fl oz/2 cups) water

1 tablespoon lemon juice

1 tablespoon rosewater

makes
16

Lightly grease a 16 x 26 cm (6¼ x 10½ inch) baking tin and line the base with baking paper, extending the paper over the long sides for easy removal later.

Place the semolina and bicarbonate of soda in a bowl and mix to combine. Whisk the milk, yoghurt, butter and honey in a separate bowl. Quickly, stir the milk mixture into the semolina mixture until combined. Pour into the prepared tin, smooth the top with a spatula and refrigerate for 30 minutes, or until set.

Preheat the oven to 180°C (350°F/Gas 4). Score the slice diagonally into diamond shapes. Top each diamond with an almond. Bake for 25–30 minutes, or until golden brown.

Meanwhile, place the sugar and water in a saucepan. Cook, stirring occasionally, over low heat until the sugar has dissolved. Bring to the boil, reduce the heat to low and simmer for 15 minutes, or until the syrup is thick. Stir in the lemon juice and rosewater and remove from the heat. Pour the syrup over the slice and cool in the tin. Cut into diamonds and serve.

Peanut toffee shortbread

Preheat the oven to 180°C (350°F/Gas 4). Lightly grease an 18 x 28 cm (7 x 11¼ inch) baking tin and line the base and sides with baking paper, extending the paper over the long sides for easy removal later.

Place 110 g (3¾ oz) of the butter and all the caster sugar in a large bowl and cream with electric beaters until pale and fluffy. Add the egg and beat well. Fold in the sifted flours with a large metal spoon until just combined. Press into the tin and bake for 15 minutes, or until firm and lightly coloured. Cool for 10 minutes.

Place the brown sugar, golden syrup, lemon juice and the remaining butter in a saucepan and stir over low heat until the sugar has dissolved. Simmer, stirring occasionally, for a further 5 minutes. Add the peanuts and mix well.

Spread the peanut toffee topping evenly over the base using two spoons, being careful as the mixture is very hot. Bake for 5 minutes, or until golden. Leave to slightly cool in the tin for 15 minutes, then turn out and cut into fingers while still warm.

290 g (10¼ oz) unsalted butter, softened

115 g (4 oz/½ cup) caster (superfine) sugar

1 egg

185 g (6½ oz/1½ cups) plain (all-purpose) flour, sifted

60 g (2¼ oz/½ cup) self-raising flour, sifted

185 g (6½ oz/1 cup) soft brown sugar

2 tablespoons golden syrup (light treacle)

½ teaspoon lemon juice

400 g (14 oz/2½ cups) toasted unsalted peanuts

makes
18

Pear and walnut slice

185 g (6½ oz/1½ cups) plain (all-purpose) flour

1 teaspoon baking powder

½ teaspoon ground ginger

1 teaspoon ground cinnamon

3 eggs

280 g (10 oz/1½ cups) soft brown sugar

1 teaspoon brandy

1 teaspoon natural vanilla extract

1 teaspoon finely grated orange zest

125 g (4½ oz/1 cup) walnut pieces

2 medium pears, peeled, cored and chopped

80 g (2¾ oz/½ cup) chopped raisins

icing (confectioners') sugar, sifted, for dusting

makes
18

Preheat the oven to 180°C (350°F/Gas 4). Lightly grease a 20 x 30 cm (8 x 12 inch) baking tin and line the base with baking paper, extending the paper over two long sides for easy removal later.

Sift the flour, baking powder, ginger and cinnamon onto a sheet of baking paper. Beat the eggs, brown sugar, brandy and vanilla extract in a large bowl for 3 minutes, or until pale and creamy, then add the orange zest. Fold the dry ingredients into the egg mixture with a large metal spoon. Add the walnuts, pear and raisins and gently mix.

Spread the mixture into the prepared tin and smooth the top with a spatula. Bake for 35–40 minutes, or until a skewer inserted in the centre comes out clean. Cool in the tin. Slice into pieces and serve dusted with the icing sugar.

Raspberry mascarpone trifle slice

375 g (13 oz) jam rollettes

60 ml (2 fl oz/¼ cup) amaretto

125 g (4½ oz) mascarpone cheese

80 g (2¾ oz/⅓ cup) caster (superfine) sugar

2 eggs, separated

200 g (7 oz) white chocolate, grated

300 g (10½ oz) raspberries

thick (double/heavy) cream, to serve (optional)

makes
12

Lightly grease a 16 x 26 cm (6¼ x 10½ inch) baking tin and line the base and sides with baking paper, extending the paper over the long sides for easy removal later.

Slice each rollette into four thin rounds. Place the slices, cut-side-down, close together in the prepared tin. Press down lightly to ensure the base of the tin is covered. Sprinkle over the amaretto.

Place the mascarpone, sugar and egg yolks in a medium bowl and mix to combine—do not overmix.

Beat the egg whites in a separate bowl until soft peaks form. Fold the egg whites and the chocolate into the mascarpone mixture using a large metal spoon. Spread onto the base and smooth the surface with a spatula. Cover and place in the refrigerator for 2 hours, or until firm. Sprinkle on the raspberries. Cut into pieces and serve with cream, if desired.

Raspberry cheesecake brownies

250 g (9 oz) milk chocolate, chopped

200 g (7 oz) unsalted butter, softened

185 g (6½ oz/1 cup) soft brown sugar

4 eggs

60 g (2¼ oz/½ cup) self-raising flour, sifted

30 g (1 oz/¼ cup) unsweetened cocoa powder, sifted

250 g (9 oz/1 cup) cream cheese, at room temperature

55 g (2 oz/¼ cup) caster (superfine) sugar

125 g (4½ oz/1 cup) frozen raspberries

makes
20

Preheat the oven to 170°C (325°F/Gas 3). Lightly grease a 16 x 26 cm (6¼ x 10½ inch) baking tin and line the base with baking paper, extending the paper over the long sides for easy removal later.

Place the chocolate in a heatproof bowl. Half-fill a saucepan with water, bring to the boil and remove from the heat. Place the bowl over the saucepan, ensuring the base of the bowl doesn't touch the water. Stir occasionally until the chocolate has melted. Cool slightly.

Beat the butter and the brown sugar in a large bowl using electric beaters until thick and creamy. Add three of the eggs, one at a time, beating well after each addition. Fold in the flour and cocoa. Fold in the cooled chocolate and set aside.

Clean the electric beaters and beat the cream cheese and caster sugar in a bowl until combined. Add the remaining egg and beat well. Fold in the raspberries.

Place alternate layers of the chocolate mixture and cream cheese mixture in the tin. Use a skewer to swirl through the mixture to create a marbled effect. Bake for 50 minutes, or until firm. Cool completely in the tin before cutting into squares.

Passionfruit and lemon delicious slice

125 g (4½ oz/½ cup) unsalted butter, softened

60 g (2¼ oz/½ cup) icing (confectioners')
  sugar, sifted

½ teaspoon natural vanilla extract

185 g (6½ oz/1½ cups) plain (all-purpose)
  flour, sifted

1 teaspoon finely grated lemon zest

Filling

100 g (3½ oz) plain (all-purpose) flour

½ teaspoon baking powder

65 g (2¼ oz/¾ cup) desiccated coconut

3 eggs

230 g (8¼ oz/1 cup) caster (superfine) sugar

170 g (6 oz) tin passionfruit pulp

2 tablespoons lemon juice

1 teaspoon finely grated lemon zest

makes
18

Preheat the oven to 180°C (350°F/Gas 4). Lightly grease an 18 x 28 cm (7 x 11¼ inch) baking tin and line the base with baking paper, extending the paper over the long sides for easy removal later.

Cream the butter, sugar and vanilla in a medium bowl using electric beaters until pale and fluffy. Fold in the flour and lemon zest with a large metal spoon. Press into the prepared tin and bake for 15–20 minutes, or until lightly golden.

To make the filling, sift the flour and baking powder into a bowl, add the coconut and mix to combine. Lightly beat the eggs and sugar in a separate bowl, then add the passionfruit pulp, lemon juice and zest. Add the dry ingredients and mix well. Pour over the base and bake for 20 minutes, or until firm to touch. Cool in the tin. Cut into pieces and serve.

Rum and raisin slice

30 g (1 oz/¼ cup) raisins

80 ml (2½ fl oz/⅓ cup) dark rum

200 g (7 oz) dark chocolate, chopped

60 g (2¼ oz/¼ cup) unsalted butter, chopped

115 g (4 oz/½ cup) caster (superfine) sugar

230 ml (7¾ fl oz) thick (double/heavy) cream

125 g (4½ oz/1 cup) plain (all-purpose) flour

3 eggs, lightly beaten

unsweetened cocoa powder, sifted, for dusting

makes
30

Preheat the oven to 180°C (350°F/Gas 4). Lightly grease an 18 x 28 cm (7 x 11¼ inch) baking tin and line the base with baking paper, extending the paper over the long sides for easy removal later.

Combine the raisins and rum in a small bowl and set aside to soak.

Place the chocolate and butter in a heatproof bowl. Half-fill a saucepan with water, bring to the boil and then remove from the heat. Place the bowl over the saucepan, making sure the base of the bowl doesn't touch the water. Allow to stand, stirring occasionally, until melted. Stir in the sugar and cream and set aside to cool slightly.

Sift the flour into a large bowl. Add the rum and raisin mixture, chocolate mixture and egg, mixing well. Pour into the prepared tin and smooth the surface with a spatula. Bake for 25–30 minutes, or until just set. Cool completely, then refrigerate overnight before cutting into small pieces. Dust liberally with cocoa powder and serve.

Apple and berry slice

Preheat the oven to 180°C (350°F/Gas 4). Lightly grease a 20 x 30 cm (8 x 12 inch) baking tin and line the base with baking paper, extending the paper over two long sides for easy removal later.

Cream the butter and sugar in a large bowl using electric beaters until pale and fluffy. Add the eggs, one at a time, beating well after each addition. In a separate bowl, combine the buttermilk and vanilla. Alternately stir in the flour and the buttermilk mixture. Mix until smooth. Spread a 5 mm (¼ inch) layer in the prepared tin.

Arrange the apple on the base. Spoon the remaining mixture over the apple, smooth the surface with a spatula and scatter the berries over the top. Bake on the middle shelf in the oven for 40 minutes, or until cooked and golden. Cool in the tin for 30 minutes before lifting onto a wire rack to cool completely. Dust with icing sugar, if using, and cut into squares.

150 g (5½ oz) unsalted butter, softened

310 g (11 oz/1⅓ cups) caster (superfine) sugar

2 eggs

170 ml (5½ fl oz/⅔ cup) buttermilk

1 teaspoon natural vanilla extract

250 g (9 oz/2 cups) self-raising flour, sifted

2 large apples, peeled, cored and thinly sliced

150 g (5½ oz) blueberries

150 g (5½ oz) blackberries

icing (confectioners') sugar, sifted, for dusting
   (optional)

makes
16

Rhubarb and raspberry crumble slice

185 g (6½ oz/1½ cups) plain (all-purpose) flour

150 g (5½ oz) unsalted butter, chilled and cut into cubes

80 g (2¾ oz/⅓ cup) caster (superfine) sugar

1 egg

cream, to serve (optional)

Topping

2 green apples, peeled, cored and chopped

2 bunches rhubarb, about 1 kg (2 lb 4 oz) in total, washed, trimmed and cut into 5 cm (2 inch) lengths

55 g (2 oz/¼ cup) sugar

125 g (4½ oz/1 cup) plain (all-purpose) flour

125 g (4½ oz/½ cup) unsalted butter

80 g (2¾ oz/⅓ cup) caster (superfine) sugar

200 g (7 oz/¼ cup) blanched almonds

125 g (4½ oz/1 cup) raspberries

makes
15

Preheat the oven to 170°C (325°F/Gas 3). Lightly grease a 16 x 26 cm (6¼ x 10½ inch) baking tin and line the base with baking paper, extending the paper over the long sides for easy removal later.

Place the flour, butter and sugar in the bowl of a food processor and process until the mixture resembles breadcrumbs. Add the egg and pulse in short bursts until just combined. Press into the tin and refrigerate for 15 minutes. Transfer to the oven and bake for 15 minutes, or until pale golden. Set aside to cool.

To make the topping, place the apple, rhubarb and sugar in a medium saucepan and cook, covered, over low heat for 15 minutes, or until soft. Transfer to a bowl and allow to cool. Place the flour, butter, caster sugar and almonds in the cleaned bowl of the food processor and process to combine. Set aside 1 cup of the almond mixture. Fold the remaining mixture into the apple and rhubarb. Add the raspberries. Spoon the mixture over the base and smooth the surface with a spatula. Scatter the reserved almond filling over the top to form the crumble.

Bake for 40 minutes, or until golden. Set aside to cool slightly, then lift out of the tin, cut into pieces and serve warm, if desired, with the cream.

Apple tatin slice with brown sugar cream

3 fuji apples, peeled
60 g (2¼ oz/¼ cup) unsalted butter, chopped
115 g (4 oz/½ cup) caster (superfine) sugar
1 sheet ready-made puff pastry

Brown sugar cream
300 ml (10½ fl oz) thick (double/heavy) cream
2 tablespoons soft brown sugar

makes
8

Preheat the oven to 220°C (425°F/Gas 7). Lightly grease a 20 cm (8 inch) square baking tin and line the base and sides with baking paper, extending the paper over two opposite sides for easy removal later.

Quarter the apples and remove the cores. Cut each quarter into three wedges.

Melt the butter in a saucepan. Add the sugar and apple and cook, stirring occasionally, for 25 minutes, or until caramelised. Quickly pour into the prepared tin and spread with a spatula to cover the base.

Trim the puff pastry to 22 cm (8½ inches) square, place over the apple mixture, tucking the edges of the pastry down the inside of the tin and bake for 20–25 minutes, or until the pastry is golden. Allow to stand for 5 minutes before carefully turning the apple tatin out of the tin.

To make the brown sugar cream, gently whisk the cream and sugar in a small bowl until combined.

Cut the warm apple tatin into pieces and serve immediately with the brown sugar cream.

Dulce de leche slice

Caramel
2 x 400 g (14 oz) tins condensed milk
2 tablespoons dark rum
50 g (1¾ oz) unsalted butter

185 g (6½ oz/1 cup) soft brown sugar
220 g (7¾ oz/1¾ cups) plain (all-purpose) flour
45 g (1⅔ oz/½ cup) desiccated coconut
1 teaspoon baking powder
1 egg
1 teaspoon natural vanilla extract
180 g (6¼ oz) unsalted butter
200 g (7 oz) milk chocolate, chopped
20 g (¾ oz) Copha (white vegetable shortening),
  chopped

makes
15

To make the caramel, combine the condensed milk, rum and butter in a saucepan. Cook over low–medium heat, stirring constantly, for 15 minutes, or until a light caramel colour. Remove from the heat and set aside.

Preheat the oven to 200°C (400°F/Gas 6). Lightly grease a 16 x 26 cm (6¼ x 10½ inch) baking tin and line the base and sides with baking paper, extending the paper over the long sides for easy removal later.

Place the sugar, flour, coconut, baking powder, egg and vanilla in the bowl of a food processor and pulse in short bursts to combine. Cook the butter in a saucepan over medium heat for 6–8 minutes, or until light brown and nutty. Quickly add to the flour mixture and process until just combined. Press half the flour mixture into the prepared tin. Pour on the caramel, then sprinkle over the remaining flour mixture. Bake on the lowest shelf of the oven for 10 minutes. Transfer to a higher shelf and bake for 10–15 minutes, until golden. Allow to cool in the tin.

Place the chocolate and Copha in a heatproof bowl over a saucepan of simmering water, making sure the base of the bowl doesn't touch the water. Cook, stirring occasionally, until the chocolate has melted. Spread over the slice. Refrigerate until the chocolate has set. Cut into pieces and serve.

Nutmeg slice

Preheat the oven to 180°C (350°F/Gas 4). Lightly grease a 20 cm (8 inch) square baking tin and line the base with baking paper, extending the paper over two opposite sides for easy removal later.

Place the flour, nutmeg, cardamom, baking powder and sugar in the bowl of a food processor. Process until combined. Add the butter and pulse in short bursts until the mixture resembles breadcrumbs. Transfer 1½ cups of the mixture to the tin and press down using your fingertips.

Transfer the remaining mixture to a bowl. Add the combined bicarbonate of soda and milk along with the egg and walnuts. Mix well, pour into the tin and spread over the base using a spatula.

Bake for 50 minutes, or until the top springs back when pressed lightly. Cover the slice with foil if the top browns too quickly. Allow to cool in the tin for 10 minutes, then lift onto a wire rack to cool completely before cutting into squares to serve.

250 g (9 oz/2 cups) plain (all-purpose) flour

2 teaspoons freshly grated nutmeg

¼ teaspoon ground cardamom

½ teaspoon baking powder

280 g (10 oz/1½ cups) soft brown sugar

125 g (4½ oz/½ cup) unsalted butter, roughly chopped

1 teaspoon bicarbonate of soda (baking soda)

185 ml (6 fl oz/¾ cup) milk

1 egg, lightly beaten

185 g (6½ oz/1½ cups) roughly chopped walnuts

makes
16

Cinnamon cherry slice

250 g (9 oz/2 cups) self-raising flour

1 heaped teaspoon ground cinnamon

370 g (13 oz/2 cups) soft brown sugar

125 g (4½ oz/½ cup) unsalted butter, chilled

720 g (1 lb 9½ oz) jar pitted morello
   cherries, drained

1 teaspoon baking powder

1 egg

300 ml (10½ fl oz) cream

1 tablespoon lemon juice

makes
18

Preheat the oven to 180°C (350°F/Gas 4). Lightly grease a 20 x 30 cm (8 x 12 inch) baking tin and line the base with baking paper, extending the paper over two long sides for easy removal later.

Sift the flour and cinnamon into a medium bowl and stir in the sugar. Transfer half the mixture to another bowl. Working quickly, coarsely grate the butter and divide between the bowls. Rub in the butter with your fingertips until the mixture resembles fine breadcrumbs. Press the contents of one bowl into the prepared tin and bake for 10 minutes, or until light golden. Spread the cherries evenly over the base.

Add the baking powder to the reserved flour mixture and mix well. Lightly whisk the egg, cream and lemon juice in a separate bowl. Add the flour mixture, stirring well with a large metal spoon. Spread over the cherries and bake for 40 minutes, or until a skewer inserted in the centre comes out clean. Allow to cool in the tin, then cut into pieces.

high tea

Cookies

Cinnamon chocolate kisses

250 g (9 oz/1 cup) unsalted butter, softened

85 g (3 oz/⅔ cup) icing (confectioners') sugar

155 g (5½ oz/1¼ cups) plain (all-purpose) flour

40 g (1½ oz/⅓ cup) cornflour (cornstarch)

30 g (1 oz/¼ cup) unsweetened cocoa powder

2½ teaspoons ground cinnamon

Chocolate ganache

80 ml (2½ fl oz/⅓ cup) cream (whipping)

120 g (4¼ oz) dark chocolate (54 per cent cocoa solids), finely chopped

makes about
50

Preheat the oven to 160°C (315°F/Gas 2–3). Line two baking trays with baking paper.

Cream the butter and sugar in a medium-sized bowl using electric beaters until pale and fluffy. Sift in the flour, cornflour, cocoa and cinnamon and beat until just combined. Spoon the mixture into a piping (icing) bag fitted with a 1 cm (½ inch) star nozzle. Pipe 3 cm (1¼ inch) stars, about 2 cm (¾ inch) apart, onto the prepared trays. Refrigerate for 20 minutes. Bake, swapping the trays halfway through cooking, for 20 minutes, or until just cooked through. Allow the biscuits to cool on the trays.

Meanwhile, to make the chocolate ganache, heat the cream in a small saucepan until almost simmering. Place the chocolate in a heatproof bowl and pour on the hot cream. Stand for 1 minute, then stir until the chocolate has melted. Cover with plastic wrap and refrigerate, stirring occasionally, for 30 minutes, or until the ganache is a thick, spreadable consistency.

Spread the base of half the biscuits with ganache and sandwich together with the remaining biscuits.

These kisses will keep, stored in an airtight container, for up to 5 days.

Fig and ginger cookies

Preheat the oven to 180°C (350°F/Gas 4). Line two baking trays with baking paper.

Cream the butter, sugar and vanilla in a medium bowl using electric beaters until pale and fluffy, then add the egg yolk and beat until just combined.

Transfer the butter mixture to a large bowl, add the figs and ginger, and stir to combine. Sift the flour into the mixture and add the bicarbonate of soda and ground ginger. Stir with a wooden spoon until a soft dough forms.

Shape tablespoons of dough into balls, place on the trays 4 cm (1½ inches) apart and flatten slightly. Bake for 10–12 minutes, or until lightly golden around the edges. Allow to cool on the trays for a few minutes, then transfer to a wire rack to cool completely. Repeat with the remaining dough.

These cookies will keep, stored in an airtight container, for up to 4 days.

160 g (5⅔ oz/⅔ cup) unsalted butter, softened

140 g (5 oz/¾ cup) soft brown sugar

1 teaspoon natural vanilla extract

1 egg yolk

95 g (3¼ oz/½ cup) chopped semi-dried figs

90 g (3¼ oz/½ cup) chopped glacé ginger

210 g (7½ oz/1¾ cups) plain (all-purpose) flour

½ teaspoon bicarbonate of soda (baking soda)

1½ tablespoons ground ginger

makes
36

Almond fruit bread

3 egg whites

125 g (4½ oz) caster (superfine) sugar

125 g (4½ oz/1 cup) plain (all-purpose) flour, sifted

125 g (4½ oz) whole almonds

100 g (3½ oz/½ cup) glacé cherries

30 g (1 oz) glacé apricots, cut into pieces the same size as the cherries

30 g (1 oz) glacé pineapple, cut into pieces the same size as the almonds

makes about
35 slices

Preheat the oven to 180°C (350°F/Gas 4). Lightly grease a 25 x 8 cm (10 x 3¼ inch) loaf (bar) tin and line it with baking paper.

Whisk the egg whites in a bowl until soft peaks form, then gradually add the sugar, whisking continuously. Continue whisking until very stiff peaks form, then fold through the flour. Gently fold in the almonds and the glacé fruits. Transfer the mixture to the prepared tin, smooth the surface and bake for 30–40 minutes, or until firm to the touch.

Cool in the tin for 10 minutes, then turn out and peel off the baking paper. Cool completely on a wire rack, then wrap in foil and set aside for 1–2 days.

Preheat the oven to 140°C (275°F/Gas 1) and line a baking tray with baking paper. Using a very sharp knife, cut the loaf into wafer-thin slices. Spread on to the baking tray and bake for 45–50 minutes, until dry and crisp. Cool on the trays for a few minutes, then transfer to a wire rack to cool completely.

Almond fruit bread will keep, stored in an airtight container, for up to 5 days.

Ginger fingers

Preheat the oven to 150°C (300°F/Gas 2). Line a large baking tray with baking paper. Lay the macadamias on another baking tray and toast for 3–5 minutes, or until lightly golden. Set aside to cool.

Cream the butter and sugar in a medium-sized bowl using electric beaters until pale and fluffy. Mix in the glacé ginger and nuts. Sift in the flours and stir with a wooden spoon to form a dough.

Gather the dough into a ball and roll out to a 1 cm (½ inch) thick rectangle. Cut into 3 x 7 cm (1¼ x 2¾ inch) fingers. Place on the tray and sprinkle with the caster sugar. Bake for 35 minutes, or until the ginger fingers are pale golden underneath. Allow to cool on the tray for a few minutes, then transfer to a wire rack to cool completely.

Ginger fingers will keep, stored in an airtight container, for up to 2 days.

100 g (3½ oz/¾ cup) chopped macadamia nuts

250 g (9 oz/1 cup) unsalted butter, softened

80 g (2¾ oz/⅓ cup) caster (superfine) sugar

100 g (3½ oz) glacé ginger, chopped

250 g (9 oz/2 cups) plain (all-purpose) flour

90 g (3¼ oz/½ cup) rice flour

caster (superfine) sugar, to sprinkle

makes
25

Pecan praline cookies

115 g (4 oz/½ cup) caster (superfine) sugar

125 g (4½ oz/½ cup) unsalted butter, softened

170 g (6 oz/¾ cup) caster (superfine) sugar, extra

1 teaspoon natural vanilla extract

1 egg yolk

250 g (9 oz/2 cups) plain (all-purpose) flour

1 teaspoon baking powder

150 g (5½ oz/1½ cups) whole pecans

makes
24

Preheat the oven to 160°C (350°F/Gas 2–3). Line two baking trays with baking paper.

To make the praline, combine the caster sugar and 1 tablespoon water in a small saucepan, stirring over low heat until the sugar is dissolved. Use a pastry brush to brush down any excess sugar on the side of the saucepan. Once the sugar is dissolved, stop stirring and cook until the liquid becomes a golden caramel colour. Pour this toffee onto one of the prepared trays, spreading it out evenly. Allow to cool and harden, then break into pieces. Process in a food processor until finely chopped. Re-line the baking tray with baking paper.

Cream the butter, extra sugar and vanilla extract in a bowl using electric beaters until pale and fluffy, then add the egg yolk, beating until just combined. Add the finely chopped praline and stir to combine. Sift in the flour and baking powder and stir with a wooden spoon to form a soft dough.

Shape tablespoons of the dough into small logs and press a pecan into the centre of each. Place on the prepared trays 4 cm (1½ inches) apart and bake for 12–15 minutes, or until lightly golden around the edges. Allow to cool on the trays for a few minutes, then transfer to a wire rack to cool completely.

These cookies will keep, stored in an airtight container, for up to 2 weeks.

Walnut and orange biscotti

310 g (11 oz/2½ cups) plain (all-purpose) flour,
plus extra for rolling

1 teaspoon baking powder

½ teaspoon bicarbonate of soda (baking soda)

170 g (6 oz/¾ cup) caster (superfine) sugar

3 eggs, lightly beaten

finely grated zest from 3 oranges

2 teaspoons natural vanilla extract

250 g (9 oz/2½ cups) walnut halves, lightly toasted
and roughly chopped

makes
40

Preheat the oven to 170°C (325°F/Gas 3). Lightly grease a baking tray.

Sift the flour, baking powder and bicarbonate of soda into a large bowl, then stir in the sugar. Combine the eggs, orange zest and vanilla in a bowl, stirring with a fork to mix well. Pour the egg mixture into the flour mixture and stir until nearly combined, then, using your hands, knead briefly to form a firm dough. Put the dough on a lightly floured work surface and knead the walnuts into the dough.

Divide the dough into three even-sized pieces. Working with one piece of dough at a time, roll to form a 29 cm (11½ inch) log. Gently pat the surface to flatten the log to a 4 cm (1½ inch) width, then place the three logs on the prepared tray and bake for 30 minutes, or until light golden and firm. Remove from the oven and cool for 15 minutes.

Reduce the oven to 150°C (300°F/Gas 2). When the logs are cool enough to handle, cut them on the diagonal into 1 cm (½ inch) thick slices and arrange in a single layer on two baking trays and bake for 15 minutes, or until the biscotti are dry, swapping the position of the trays halfway through cooking. Cool on a wire rack.

Biscotti will keep, stored in an airtight container, for up to 3 weeks.

high tea

Cookies

Chocolate shortbread

150 g (5½ oz/1 cup) chopped dark chocolate
250 g (9 oz/1 cup) unsalted butter, softened
115 g (4 oz/½ cup) caster (superfine) sugar
310 g (11 oz/2½ cups) plain (all-purpose) flour
2 tablespoons unsweetened cocoa powder
1 tablespoon drinking chocolate

makes
65

Preheat the oven to 160°C (315°F/Gas 2–3). Lightly grease two baking trays.

Place the chocolate in a heatproof bowl over a saucepan of simmering water, ensuring the bowl doesn't touch the water. Stir until the chocolate has melted. Set aside to cool for 5 minutes.

Cream the butter and sugar in a medium bowl using electric beaters until pale and fluffy, then add the melted chocolate. Sift in the flour and stir with a wooden spoon to form a soft dough.

Shape tablespoons of the dough into balls, place on the trays well apart and flatten slightly. Bake for 12–15 minutes. Allow to cool on the trays for a few minutes, then completely cool on a wire rack. Repeat with the remaining dough.

Just before serving, sift the combined cocoa and drinking chocolate over the shortbread to dust.

These shortbreads will keep, stored in an airtight container, for up to 1 week.

Spicy apple drops

2 eggs

60 g (2¼ oz/¼ cup) unsalted butter,
  melted and cooled

220 g (7¾ oz/1 cup) raw (demerara) sugar

30 g (1 oz/¼ cup) malted milk powder

280 g (10 oz/2¼ cups) self-raising flour

1 teaspoon ground cinnamon

½ teaspoon ground mixed spice

200 g (7 oz) green apple, peeled, cored and
  chopped (about 1½ apples)

140 g (5 oz/3⅓ cups) cornflakes

60 g (2¼ oz/½ cup) chopped pecans

icing (confectioners') sugar, to dust

ground cinnamon, to dust

makes
20

Preheat the oven to 180°C (350°F/Gas 4). Lightly grease two baking trays and line with baking paper.

Using electric beaters, lightly beat the eggs in a medium bowl. Stir in the melted butter, add the sugar and then beat until smooth. Sift the malted milk powder, flour, ¼ teaspoon salt, cinnamon and the mixed spice into the mixture and beat well. Stir in the apple, cornflakes and pecans and mix well.

Shape tablespoons of the dough into balls and place well apart on the trays. Bake for 15–20 minutes, or until lightly golden. Allow to cool on the trays for a few minutes, then transfer to a wire rack to cool completely. When the cookies are cool, dust with the sifted icing sugar and then sprinkle a little cinnamon on top.

These cookies will keep, stored in an airtight container, for up to 5 days.

Classic shortbread

225 g (8 oz) unsalted butter, softened

115 g (4 oz/½ cup) caster (superfine) sugar,
   plus extra for dusting

210 g (7½ oz/1¾ cups) plain (all-purpose) flour

115 g (4 oz/⅔ cup) rice flour

makes
16 pieces

Lightly grease two baking trays. Cream the butter and sugar in a medium bowl using electric beaters until pale and fluffy. Sift in the flours and a pinch of salt and stir with a wooden spoon until it resembles fine breadcrumbs. Transfer to a lightly floured work surface and knead gently to form a soft dough. Cover with plastic wrap and refrigerate for 30 minutes.

Preheat the oven to 190°C (375°F/Gas 5). Divide the dough in half and roll out one half onto a lightly floured work surface to form a 20 cm (8 inch) round. Carefully transfer to one of the trays. Using a sharp knife, score the surface of the dough into eight equal wedges, prick the surface lightly with a fork and, using your fingers, press the edge to form a fluted effect. Repeat using the remaining dough to make a second round. Lightly dust the shortbreads with the extra sugar.

Bake for 18–20 minutes, or until the shortbreads are lightly golden. Remove from the oven and while still hot, follow the score marks and cut into wedges. Cool on the baking trays for 5 minutes, then transfer to a wire rack.

These shortbreads will keep, stored in an airtight container, for up to 1 week.

TIP While shortbread can be made with plain flour alone, adding rice flour produces a lighter result.

Molasses moons

Cream the butter and sugar in a medium bowl using electric beaters until pale and fluffy, then add the molasses and egg yolk, beating until just combined. Sift in the flour, bicarbonate of soda and mixed spice and stir with a wooden spoon to form a soft dough. Cover with plastic wrap and refrigerate for 2 hours.

Preheat the oven to 160°C (315°F/Gas 2–3). Line two baking trays with baking paper.

Divide the dough in half and roll each between two pieces of baking paper to 5 mm (¼ inch) thick. Cut the dough into moon shapes using a 6 cm (2½ inch) moon-shaped cutter, re-rolling the scraps and cutting more moons. Place on the prepared trays 5 cm (2 inches) apart and bake for 7 minutes. Allow to cool on the trays for a few minutes, then transfer to a wire rack to cool completely. Repeat with the remaining dough.

Molasses moons will keep, stored in an airtight container, for up to 3 weeks.

125 g (4½ oz/½ cup) unsalted butter, softened

185 g (6½ oz/1 cup) soft brown sugar

2 tablespoons molasses

1 egg yolk

250 g (9 oz/2 cups) plain (all-purpose) flour

½ teaspoon bicarbonate of soda (baking soda)

1 teaspoon ground mixed spice

makes
60

Apricot cookies with lemon icing

160 g (5⅔ oz/⅔ cup) unsalted butter, softened

170 g (6 oz/¾ cup) caster (superfine) sugar

2 tablespoons marmalade

1 teaspoon natural vanilla extract

200 g (7 oz) dried apricots, chopped

125 g (4½ oz/1 cup) self-raising flour

40 g (1½ oz/⅓ cup) plain (all-purpose) flour

Icing

125 g (4½ oz/1 cup) icing (confectioners') sugar

2 teaspoons lemon juice

makes
32

Line two baking trays with baking paper. Cream the butter and sugar in a medium bowl using electric beaters until light and creamy. Add the marmalade, vanilla and apricots and mix until well combined.

Sift the flours into a large bowl and then stir in the butter mixture. Turn onto a lightly floured surface and bring together until just smooth. Divide in half. Place each portion on a sheet of baking paper and roll up in the paper to form two logs, 21 cm (8¼ inches) long and 4.5 cm (1¾ inches) thick. Lay on a tray and refrigerate for 15 minutes until firm.

Preheat the oven to 180°C (350°F/Gas 4). Remove the baking paper and, using a serrated knife, cut the logs into 1 cm (½ inch) diagonal slices. Place well apart on the prepared trays. Bake for 10–15 minutes, or until golden. Allow to cool on the trays for at least 5 minutes, then cool completely on a wire rack. Repeat with the remaining dough.

To make the icing, sift the icing sugar into a small bowl. Add the lemon juice and 3 teaspoons hot water and stir until smooth. Place in a small paper or plastic piping bag. Seal the end and snip off the tip. Decorate the cookies with the icing.

These cookies will keep, stored in an airtight container, for up to 5 days.

Custard dream stars

185 g (6½ oz/¾ cup) unsalted butter, softened
40 g (1½ oz/⅓ cup) icing (confectioners') sugar
1 teaspoon natural vanilla extract
125 g (4½ oz/1 cup) plain (all-purpose) flour
40 g (1½ oz/⅓ cup) custard powder
small sugar decorations

makes
30

Preheat the oven to 180°C (350°F/Gas 4). Line two baking trays with baking paper.

Cream the butter, sugar and vanilla in a medium bowl using electric beaters until pale and fluffy. Sift in the flour and custard powder and stir with a wooden spoon to form a soft dough, being careful not to over mix.

Transfer the mixture to a piping bag fitted with a 1.5 cm (⅝ inch) star nozzle. Pipe the mixture well apart onto the prepared trays to form star shapes, about 4 cm (1½ inches) in diameter. Place a sugar decoration in the centre of each star. Refrigerate for 20 minutes.

Bake for 12–15 minutes, or until lightly golden, taking care not to burn. Cool on the trays for a few minutes, then transfer to a wire rack to cool completely.

Custard dream stars will keep, stored in an airtight container, for up to 5 days.

NOTE You can buy small sugar decorations from most delicatessens and supermarkets.

Almond and coffee meringue hearts

3 egg whites

335 g (11¾ oz/2⅔ cups) icing (confectioners')
   sugar, sifted, plus extra for dusting

½ teaspoon lemon juice

finely grated zest of ½ lemon

200 g (7 oz/2 cups) ground almonds

1 teaspoon ground cinnamon

2 teaspoons finely ground espresso coffee beans

makes
40

Place the egg whites in a large bowl and beat using electric beaters until stiff peaks form. Gradually add the sugar, a spoonful at a time, and beat until the sugar has dissolved and the meringue mixture is thick and glossy. Whisk in the lemon juice. Remove 150 g (5½ oz/1 cup) of the meringue mixture and set aside.

Combine the lemon zest, ground almonds, cinnamon and ground coffee in a separate bowl and gently fold into the meringue mixture to form a thick dough. Refrigerate for 1 hour, or until the dough is firm.

Preheat the oven to 180°C (350°F/Gas 4). Line two baking trays with baking paper.

Dust a clean work surface with the extra sugar and roll out the dough to 8 mm (⅜ inch) thick. Cut out the dough using a lightly greased 5 cm (2 inch) heart-shaped cookie cutter and transfer to the prepared trays. Place a teaspoonful of the reserved meringue mixture on top of each biscuit shape and spread out using the back of a spoon or a small spatula. Set aside for 15 minutes to dry out the meringue. Bake for 10–12 minutes, or until light golden brown around the edges. Transfer to a wire rack to cool completely.

Pineapple and coconut cookies

160 g (5⅔ oz/⅔ cup) unsalted butter, softened

230 g (8¼ oz/1 cup) caster (superfine) sugar

1 teaspoon natural vanilla extract

1 egg

2 tablespoons milk

1 teaspoon finely grated lemon zest

95 g (3¼ oz/½ cup) glacé pineapple,
   finely sliced

250 g (9 oz/2 cups) plain (all-purpose) flour

1 teaspoon baking powder

45 g (1⅔ oz/½ cup) desiccated coconut

30 g (1 oz/½ cup) shredded coconut, plus extra
   to garnish

makes
36

Preheat the oven to 180°C (350°F/Gas 4). Line two baking trays with baking paper.

Cream the butter, sugar and vanilla in a bowl using electric beaters until pale and fluffy, then add the egg, milk and grated lemon zest, beating until just combined. Transfer the mixture to a large bowl, add the glacé pineapple and stir to combine. Sift the flour into the mixture and add the baking powder and coconuts, and stir with a wooden spoon until a soft dough forms.

Shape tablespoons of the dough into balls and place on the trays 4 cm (1½ inches) apart. Sprinkle the extra coconut on the cookies and flatten slightly to make 5 cm (2 inch) rounds. Bake for 13 minutes, or until lightly golden around the edges. Cool for a few minutes on the trays, then transfer to a wire rack to cool completely. Repeat with the remaining dough.

These cookies will keep, stored in an airtight container, for up to 5 days.

Lemon curd sandwiches

Lemon curd

juice from 2 lemons

80 g (2¾ oz/⅓ cup) caster (superfine) sugar

3 teaspoons cornflour (cornstarch)

4 egg yolks

finely grated zest from 1 lemon

110 g (3¾ oz) unsalted butter, softened

115 g (4 oz/½ cup) caster (superfine) sugar

½ teaspoon natural vanilla extract

2 teaspoons finely grated lemon zest

1 egg yolk

155 g (5½ oz/1¼ cups) plain (all-purpose) flour

30 g (1 oz/¼ cup) icing (confectioners') sugar,
   for dusting

makes
24

To make the lemon curd, combine the lemon juice, sugar and the cornflour in a small saucepan and, over low heat, whisk until combined. Slowly bring to the boil, stirring with a wooden spoon until the mixture thickens. Remove from the heat and whisk in the egg yolks and lemon zest. Return to a gentle heat and cook for 2–3 minutes, stirring until well combined and thickened. Remove from the heat and place the curd in a heatproof bowl. Place plastic wrap on the surface of the curd to stop a skin forming and set aside to cool. The lemon curd can be made in advance, and needs to be refrigerated.

Preheat the oven to 170°C (325°F/Gas 3). Line two baking trays with baking paper.

Cream the butter, sugar and vanilla in a bowl using electric beaters until pale and fluffy, then add the lemon zest and egg yolk, beating until just combined. Sift in the flour and, using a wooden spoon, stir until it forms a soft dough. Turn out the dough, and gently shape it into a flat disc. Cover with plastic wrap and refrigerate for 20 minutes.

Roll the dough out between two pieces of baking paper to 3 mm (⅛ inch) thick. Cut dough into round and ring shapes, using a 4.5 cm (1¾ inch) round-shaped cutter and a 4.5 cm (1¾ inch) ring-shaped cutter so you end up with the same amount of each shape. Re-roll any leftover dough scraps and cut more rounds and rings.

Place on the trays 3 cm (1¼ inches) apart and bake for 9 minutes, or until lightly golden around the edges. Allow to cool on the trays for a few minutes, then transfer to a wire rack to cool completely.

On the cookie rounds, place a teaspoon of the lemon curd, flatten a little with a knife and then sandwich it together with a ring cookie, pressing down so the curd goes right to the edge. Dust the cookies with the icing sugar. Repeat with the remaining cookies.

Filled cookies will keep, in an airtight container, for 3 days. Unfilled cookies will keep, stored in an airtight container, for 3 weeks. (For image, see page 184.)

Gingerbread

350 g (12 oz) plain (all-purpose) flour

2 teaspoons baking powder

2 teaspoons ground ginger

100 g (3½ oz) unsalted butter, chilled and diced

140 g (5 oz/¾ cup) soft brown sugar

1 egg, beaten

115 g (4 oz/⅓ cup) dark treacle

silver balls (optional)

Icing glaze

1 egg white

3 teaspoons lemon juice

155 g (5½ oz/1¼ cups) icing (confectioners') sugar

Royal icing

1 egg white

200 g (7 oz) icing (confectioners') sugar

makes about
40

Preheat the oven to 190°C (375°F/Gas 5). Lightly grease two baking trays.

Sift the flour, baking powder, ground ginger and a pinch of salt into a bowl. Rub in the butter with your fingertips until the mixture resembles fine breadcrumbs, then stir in the sugar. Make a well in the centre, add the egg and treacle and, using a wooden spoon, stir until a soft dough forms. Knead on a clean surface until smooth.

Divide the dough in half and roll out on a lightly floured work surface until 5 mm (¼ inch) thick. Using various-shaped cookie cutters (hearts, stars or flowers), cut the dough and then transfer to the prepared trays. Bake in batches for 8 minutes, or until the gingerbread is light brown. Allow to cool on the trays for a few minutes, then transfer to a wire rack to cool completely. (If using the gingerbread as hanging decorations, use a skewer to make a small hole in each one while still hot.)

To make the icing glaze, whisk the egg white with the lemon juice until foamy, then whisk in the icing sugar to form a smooth, thin icing. Cover the surface with plastic wrap until needed. To make the royal icing, lightly whisk the egg white until just foamy, then gradually whisk in enough icing sugar to form a soft icing. Cover surface with plastic wrap until needed.

Brush a thin layer of icing glaze over some of the gingerbread and leave to set. Using an icing bag filled with royal icing, decorate the gingerbread as shown in the photograph on page 185, or as desired.

Gingerbread will keep, stored in an airtight container, for up to 3 days.

TIP To make a paper icing bag, cut a piece of baking paper into a 19 cm (7½ inch) square and then cut in half diagonally to form two triangles. Hold the triangle, with the longest side away from you, and curl the left hand point over and in towards the centre. Repeat with the right hand point, forming a cone shape, with both ends meeting neatly in the middle. Staple together at the wide end.

Cardamom crescents

60 g (2¼ oz/½ cup) slivered almonds

250 g (9 oz/1 cup) unsalted butter, softened

3 tablespoons icing (confectioners') sugar, sifted

2 tablespoons brandy

1 teaspoon finely grated lime zest

310 g (11 oz/2½ cups) plain (all-purpose) flour

1 teaspoon ground cardamom

icing (confectioners') sugar, extra, to dust and
   to store (optional)

makes
30

Preheat the oven to 180°C (350°F/Gas 4). Line two baking trays with baking paper. Put the almonds on another baking tray and bake for 5 minutes, or until lightly golden. Allow to cool and finely chop.

Cream the butter and sugar in a medium bowl using electric beaters until pale and fluffy, then mix in the brandy, lime zest and the toasted almonds. Sift in the flour and cardamom and stir with a wooden spoon to form a soft dough.

Shape tablespoons of the dough into small crescents and place on the prepared trays well apart. Bake for 15–20 minutes, or until lightly golden. Allow to cool on the trays for a few minutes, then transfer to a wire rack to cool completely.

To serve, sift over some of the icing sugar to cover the crescents completely. If storing the crescents, place in a tin or plastic box and cover entirely with the remaining icing sugar.

The crescents will keep, stored in an airtight container, for up to 5 days.

Orange polenta cookies

Preheat the oven to 200°C (400°F/Gas 6). Line two baking trays with baking paper.

Combine the butter, sugar, orange flower water and orange zest in a food processor and process until the mixture is light and creamy. Add the eggs and process until smooth. Add the flour and polenta and pulse until a sticky dough forms.

Transfer the mixture to a piping bag fitted with a 2 cm (¾ inch) star nozzle. Pipe on to the prepared baking trays to form 7 cm (2¾ inch) crescents. Bake for 15 minutes, or until lightly golden around the edges. Cool on the trays for a few minutes, then transfer to onto a wire rack to cool completely.

Orange polenta biscuits will keep, stored in an airtight container, for up to 3 days.

125 g (4½ oz/½ cup) unsalted butter, softened
80 g (2¾ oz/⅓ cup) caster (superfine) sugar
1 teaspoon orange flower water
finely grated zest from 1 orange
2 eggs
165 g (5¾ oz/1⅓ cups) plain (all-purpose) flour
80 g (2¾ oz/½ cup) polenta

makes about
20

Honey jumbles

Preheat the oven to 180°C (350°F/Gas 4). Line two baking trays with baking paper.

Cream the butter and sugars in a medium bowl using electric beaters until pale and fluffy, then add the honey, egg yolk and vanilla, beating until just combined. Sift in the flour and bicarbonate of soda and stir with a wooden spoon to form a soft dough.

Shape tablespoons of the dough into logs, place on the trays 5 cm (2 inches) apart and flatten slightly. Bake for 10 minutes, or until lightly golden around the edges. Cool on the trays for a few minutes, then transfer to a wire rack to cool completely.

To make the icing, place the icing sugar in a medium bowl. Add enough lemon juice to make a smooth and spreadable consistency. Once the jumbles are completely cooled, spread the tops with the icing.

Honey jumbles will keep, stored in an airtight container, for up to 3 weeks.

125 g (4½ oz/½ cup) unsalted butter, softened

55 g (2 oz/¼ cup) caster (superfine) sugar

45 g (1¾ oz/¼ cup) soft brown sugar

115 g (4 oz/⅓ cup) honey

1 egg yolk

1 teaspoon natural vanilla extract

250 g (9 oz/2 cups) plain (all-purpose) flour

½ teaspoon bicarbonate of soda (baking soda)

125 g (4½ oz/1 cup) icing (confectioners') sugar

1–2 tablespoons lemon juice

makes
24

Florentines

55 g (2 oz) unsalted butter

45 g (1¾ oz/¼ cup) soft brown sugar

2 teaspoons honey

25 g (1 oz/¼ cup) flaked almonds, roughly chopped

2 tablespoons chopped dried apricots

2 tablespoons chopped glacé cherries

2 tablespoons mixed candied citrus peel

40 g (1½ oz/⅓ cup) plain (all-purpose) flour, sifted

120 g (4¼ oz) chopped dark chocolate

makes
12

Preheat the oven to 180°C (350°F/Gas 4). Grease and line two baking trays with baking paper.

Mix the butter, brown sugar and honey in a saucepan over low heat until the butter is melted and all the ingredients are combined. Remove from the heat and add the almonds, apricots, glacé cherries, mixed peel and the flour. Mix well.

Shape tablespoons of the dough into balls, place on the prepared trays well apart and flatten into 5 cm (2 inch) rounds. Bake for 10 minutes, or until lightly browned. Cool on the trays for a few minutes, then transfer to a wire rack to cool completely.

Place the chocolate in a small heatproof bowl over a saucepan of simmering water, ensuring the bowl doesn't touch the water. Stir until the chocolate has melted. Spread the melted chocolate on the bottom of each florentine and, using a fork, make a wavy pattern on the chocolate before it sets. Leave the chocolate to set before serving.

Florentines will keep, stored in an airtight container, for up to 5 days.

Lemon stars

125 g (4½ oz/½ cup) unsalted butter, cubed
   and softened
115 g (4 oz/½ cup) caster (superfine) sugar
2 egg yolks
2 teaspoons finely grated lemon zest
155 g (5½ oz/1¼ cups) plain (all-purpose) flour
110 g (3¾ oz/¾ cup) coarse polenta (cornmeal)
icing (confectioners') sugar, to dust

makes
22

Preheat the oven to 160°C (315°F/Gas 2–3). Line a baking tray with baking paper.

Cream the butter and sugar in a medium bowl using electric beaters until pale and fluffy, add the egg yolks and lemon zest, and beat until just combined. Sift in the flour, add the cornmeal and stir with a wooden spoon to form a soft dough.

Turn the dough out onto a lightly floured surface and knead gently until the mixture comes together. Roll out the dough between two pieces of baking paper to 1 cm (½ inch) thick.

Cut the dough into stars using a 3 cm (1¼ inch) star-shaped cutter, re-rolling the dough scraps and cutting more stars. Place on the prepared trays well apart and bake for 15–20 minutes, or until lightly golden around the edges. Allow to cool on the trays for a few minutes, then transfer to a wire rack, dust with icing sugar and leave to cool completely.

Lemon stars will keep, stored in an airtight container, for up to 5 days.

Maple brown sugar cookies

140 g (5 oz) unsalted butter, softened

185 g (6½ oz/1 cup) soft brown sugar

80 ml (2½ fl oz/⅓ cup) maple syrup

1 egg yolk

250 g (9 oz/2 cups) plain (all-purpose) flour

½ teaspoon bicarbonate of soda (baking soda)

¼ teaspoon ground cinnamon

¼ teaspoon ground cardamom

Maple syrup icing

125 g (4½ oz/1 cup) icing (confectioners') sugar,
  sifted

1½ tablespoons maple syrup

½ teaspoon natural vanilla extract

makes
48

Preheat the oven to 180°C (350°F/Gas 4). Line two baking trays with baking paper.

Cream the butter and sugar in a medium-sized bowl using electric beaters until pale and fluffy, then add the maple syrup and egg yolk, beating until just combined. Sift in the flour, bicarbonate of soda, cinnamon and cardamom, and stir with a wooden spoon to form a soft dough. Shape the dough into a flat disc, cover with plastic wrap and refrigerate for 20 minutes.

Roll out the dough between two pieces of baking paper to 5 mm (¼ inch) thick. Cut the dough into rings using a 5 cm (2 inch) round cookie cutter, re-rolling the dough scraps and cutting more circles. Place on the prepared trays 4 cm (1½ inches) apart and bake for 8 minutes, or until lightly golden. Allow to cool on the trays for a few minutes, then transfer to a wire rack to cool completely.

To make the maple syrup icing, place the icing sugar, maple syrup and vanilla in a medium bowl, and stir to combine. Add enough water to make a smooth, thick, runny consistency. When the cookies are completely cool, drizzle with the maple syrup icing.

These cookies will keep, stored in an airtight container, for up to 3 weeks.

Amore

250 g (9 oz/2 cups) plain (all-purpose) flour

1 teaspoon baking powder

¼ teaspoon ground mixed spice

60 g (2¼ oz/⅓ cup) soft brown sugar

½ teaspoon finely grated lemon zest

1 egg

1 tablespoon milk

1 teaspoon natural vanilla extract

100 g (3½ oz) unsalted butter, softened

2 teaspoons unsweetened cocoa powder

1 teaspoon brandy

icing (confectioners') sugar, to dust

makes
20

Preheat the oven to 170°C (325°F/Gas 3). Line two baking trays with baking paper.

Sift the flour, ¼ teaspoon salt, baking powder and mixed spice into a bowl. Add the sugar, lemon zest, egg, milk, vanilla and butter and, using electric beaters, mix into a smooth dough. Turn out onto a lightly floured surface and roll into a smooth ball. Cover with plastic wrap and refrigerate the dough for 20 minutes.

Divide the dough in half. On a lightly floured surface, roll out one portion until 3 mm (⅛ inch) thick. Cut the dough into ten hearts using a 7 cm (2¾ inch) heart-shaped cookie cutter. Re-roll out the scraps and cut out ten 1 cm (½ inch) hearts. Place on the prepared trays. Working with the other portion, knead in the cocoa and brandy until just combined, then repeat as above.

Lay a small heart onto a large heart of the opposite colour. Bake for 12 minutes, or until lightly golden. Allow to cool on the trays for a few minutes, then transfer to a wire rack to cool completely. Sift over the icing sugar.

These will keep, stored in an airtight container, for up to 5 days.

Cinnamon circles

50 g (1¾ oz) unsalted butter, softened

80 g (2¾ oz/⅓ cup) caster (superfine) sugar

½ teaspoon natural vanilla extract

85 g (3 oz/⅔ cup) plain (all-purpose) flour

1 tablespoon milk

2 tablespoons caster (superfine) sugar, extra

½ teaspoon ground cinnamon

makes
25

Preheat the oven to 180°C (350°F/Gas 4). Line two baking trays with baking paper.

Cream the butter and sugar in a medium bowl using electric beaters until pale and fluffy, then stir in the vanilla. Sift in the flour and add the milk. Stir with a wooden spoon to form a soft dough, gather into a ball and place on a sheet of baking paper.

Press the dough out to a log shape, 25 cm (10 inches) long and 3 cm (1¼ inches) thick. Roll in the paper and twist the ends to seal. Refrigerate for 20 minutes, or until firm.

Cut the log into rounds 1 cm (½ inch) thick. Sift the extra caster sugar and cinnamon onto a plate and roll each cookie in the sugar mixture, coating well. Lay well apart on the prepared trays and bake for 20 minutes, or until lightly golden around the edges. Allow to cool on the trays for a few minutes, then transfer to a wire rack to cool completely.

These cookies will keep, stored in an airtight container, for up to 5 days.

Pecan and coffee sugar cookies

40 g (1½ oz/⅓ cup) icing (confectioners') sugar

1½ tablespoons very finely ground espresso
    coffee beans

100 g (3½ oz/1 cup) pecans

55 g (2 oz/¼ cup) caster (superfine) sugar

185 g (6½ oz/¾ cup) unsalted butter, softened

1 egg yolk

200 g (7 oz/1⅔ cups) plain (all-purpose) flour

makes
45

Preheat the oven to 180°C (350°F/Gas 4). Line two baking trays with baking paper.

Combine the icing sugar and ground coffee in a bowl and set aside.

Place the pecans and 1 tablespoon of the caster sugar in the bowl of a food processor and process until the mixture resembles fine breadcrumbs.

Cream the butter and the remaining caster sugar in a large bowl using electric beaters until pale and fluffy. Add the egg yolk and beat until well combined. Stir in the ground pecan mixture, sift in the flour and a pinch of salt and mix to form a dough.

Roll pieces of the dough into 2.5 cm (1 inch) balls, place on the prepared trays and flatten slightly. Bake for 10 minutes, or until lightly golden around the edges and cooked through. Transfer to a wire rack and, while the cookies are still hot, sift the coffee mixture over the top. Set aside to cool completely.

Coffee wafers

185 g (6½ oz/¾ cup) unsalted butter, softened

170 g (6 oz/¾ cup) caster (superfine) sugar

45 g (1¾ oz/¼ cup) dark brown sugar

1 teaspoon natural vanilla extract

1 egg yolk

1 tablespoon milk

60 ml (2 fl oz/¼ cup) strong espresso coffee

375 g (13 oz/3 cups) plain (all-purpose) flour

Coffee icing

125 g (4½ oz/1 cup) icing (confectioners') sugar,
   sifted

1 tablespoon espresso coffee

coffee beans, to garnish

makes
60

Preheat the oven to 180°C (350°F/Gas 4). Line two baking trays with baking paper.

Cream the butter and sugars in a large bowl using electric beaters until pale and fluffy, then add the vanilla, egg yolk, milk and coffee, beating until just combined. Sift in the flour and stir with a wooden spoon to form a soft dough.

Turn the dough out onto a lightly floured surface and knead gently until the mixture comes together. Divide the mixture in half and roll each portion between two pieces of baking paper to 5 mm (¼ inch). Cut the dough into rounds using a 5 cm (2 inch) round cookie cutter, re-rolling the dough scraps and cutting out more rounds. Place on the prepared trays 3 cm (1¼ inches) apart and bake for 10 minutes, or until golden around the edges. Allow to cool on the trays for a few minutes, then transfer to a wire rack to cool completely. Repeat with the remaining dough.

To make the coffee icing, place the icing sugar and coffee in a small bowl and stir until smooth. Using a spoon, spread a circle of icing on top of each wafer and top with coffee beans.

These wafers will keep, stored in an airtight container, for up to 2 weeks.

Lime and sour cream cookies

Preheat the oven to 180°C (350°F/Gas 4). Line two baking trays with baking paper.

Cream the butter, sugar and vanilla in a medium bowl using electric beaters until pale and fluffy, then add the lime zest and sour cream, beating until just combined. Sift in the flour and baking powder and stir with a wooden spoon to form a soft dough.

Shape tablespoons of the mixture into balls, place on the prepared trays 5 cm (2 inches) apart and flatten slightly. Bake for 15 minutes, or until lightly golden around the edges. Allow to cool on the trays for a few minutes, then transfer to a wire rack to cool completely. Repeat with the remaining dough.

These cookies will keep, stored in an airtight container, for up to 1 week.

125 g (4½ oz/½ cup) unsalted butter, softened

230 g (8¼ oz/1 cup) caster (superfine) sugar

1 teaspoon natural vanilla extract

1½ tablespoons finely grated lime zest

90 g (3¼ oz/⅓ cup) sour cream

250 g (9 oz/2 cups) plain (all-purpose) flour

½ teaspoon baking powder

makes
30

Strawberry pecan cookies

160 g (5⅔ oz/⅔ cup) unsalted butter, softened

170 g (6 oz/¾ cup) caster (superfine) sugar

½ teaspoon natural vanilla extract

80 g (2¾ oz/⅓ cup) fresh strawberry purée

100 g (3½ oz/½ cup) dried strawberries, thinly
   sliced

80 g (2¾ oz) ground pecans

185 g (6½ oz/1½ cups) plain (all-purpose) flour

300 g (10½ oz) white chocolate, chopped

red food colouring

makes
32

Preheat the oven to 180°C (350°F/Gas 4). Line two
baking trays with baking paper.

Cream the butter, sugar and vanilla in a bowl
using electric beaters until pale and fluffy. Mix in
the strawberry purée, dried strawberries and ground
pecans. Sift in the flour and stir until the mixture
forms a soft dough.

Shape tablespoons of the dough into balls and put
on the prepared trays 5 cm (2 inches) apart. Flatten
slightly and bake for 12–15 minutes, or until lightly
golden around the edges. Allow to cool on the trays
for a few minutes, then leave to cool completely on
a wire rack.

Place the chocolate in a small heatproof bowl over
a saucepan of simmering water, ensuring the bowl
doesn't touch the water. Stir until the chocolate has
melted. Remove from the heat and stir in the food
colouring, a drop at a time, until the chocolate is
pale pink. Dip each cookie in to the chocolate to
coat half of it. Place on a lined baking tray for about
40 minutes to set.

These cookies will keep, stored in an airtight
container, for up to 1 week.

Vanilla sugar hearts

185 g (6½ oz/¾ cup) unsalted butter, softened

230 g (8½ oz/1 cup) caster (superfine) sugar

2 teaspoons natural vanilla extract

1 egg

310 g (11 oz/2½ cups) plain (all-purpose) flour

75 g (2⅔ oz/⅓ cup) white sugar

makes
36

Cream the butter, sugar and vanilla in a medium bowl using electric beaters until pale and fluffy, then add the egg, beating until just combined. Sift in the flour and stir with a wooden spoon to form a soft dough. Divide the mixture in two, shape the halves into discs, cover with plastic wrap and refrigerate for 1 hour.

Preheat the oven to 180°C (350°F/Gas 4). Line two baking trays with baking paper.

Roll the dough out between two pieces of baking paper to 5 mm (¼ inch) thick. Cut the dough into heart shapes using a 5.5 cm (2¼ inch) heart-shaped cookie cutter, re-rolling the scraps and cutting more hearts. Place on the trays 4 cm (1½ inches) apart, sprinkle with the sugar and gently press it into the dough. Bake for 8–10 minutes, or until lightly golden around the edges. Allow to cool on the trays for a few minutes, then transfer to a wire rack to cool completely.

These cookies will keep, stored in an airtight container, for up to 1 week.

Lime and coconut shortbreads

Preheat the oven to 180°C (350°F/Gas 4). Line two baking trays with baking paper.

Sift the flour and icing sugar into a bowl and stir in the coconut and lime zest. Add the butter and rub in with your fingertips until the mixture is crumbly. Add the lime juice and cut into the flour mixture using a flat-bladed knife.

Gather the dough into a ball and roll out on a lightly floured work surface to 5 mm (¼ inch) thick. Using a 5 cm (2 inch) biscuit cutter, cut into rounds. Lay well apart on the trays and bake for 15–20 minutes, or until very lightly golden. Allow to cool on the trays for a few minutes, then transfer to a wire rack to cool completely.

To make the icing, sift the extra icing sugar into a small heatproof bowl, add the extra lime juice and place over a saucepan of simmering water. Stir until smooth. Spoon a little icing onto each shortbread, stirring the icing in the bowl occasionally to prevent it from hardening, and spread evenly. Leave the shortbread on the wire rack to set.

These shortbread will keep, stored in an airtight container, for up to 5 days.

250 g (9 oz/2 cups) plain (all-purpose) flour

40 g (1½ oz/⅓ cup) icing (confectioners') sugar

65 g (2¼ oz/¾ cup) desiccated coconut

2 teaspoons finely grated lime zest

200 g (7 oz) unsalted butter, cubed and chilled

1 tablespoon lime juice

125 g (4½ oz/1 cup) icing (confectioners') sugar, extra

2 tablespoons lime juice, extra, strained

makes
25

Gingernut cookies

Preheat the oven to 170°C (325°F/Gas 3). Line two baking trays with baking paper.

Cream the butter and sugar in a medium bowl using electric beaters until pale and fluffy, then add the golden syrup and egg yolk, beating until just combined. Sift in the flour, bicarbonate of soda, ginger and mixed spice and stir with a wooden spoon until a soft dough forms.

Shape tablespoons of the dough into balls, place on the prepared trays 5 cm (2 inches) apart and flatten into 4 cm (1½ inch) rounds. Bake for 15 minutes, or until lightly golden around the edges. Cool on the trays for a few minutes, then transfer to a wire rack to cool completely.

Gingernut cookies will keep, stored in an airtight container, for up to 3 weeks.

125 g (4½ oz/½ cup) unsalted butter, softened

185 g (6½ oz/1 cup) soft brown sugar

2 tablespoons golden syrup (light treacle)

1 egg yolk

250 g (9 oz/2 cups) plain (all-purpose) flour

½ teaspoon bicarbonate of soda (baking soda)

2 teaspoons ground ginger

1 teaspoon ground mixed spice

makes
24

high tea

Chocolate delights

Real chocolate crackles

Line three 12-hole mini muffin tins with paper cases.

Combine the puffed rice and coconut in a large bowl. Place the chocolate in a heatproof bowl over a saucepan of simmering water, ensuring the bowl doesn't touch the water. Stir until the chocolate has melted. Remove from the heat.

Add the melted chocolate to the puffed rice mixture and, using a wooden spoon, stir gently until evenly combined. Spoon the mixture into the paper cases. Place in the refrigerator for 1 hour, or until set. Dust with the icing sugar if desired.

The chocolate crackles will keep, stored in an airtight container in the refrigerator, for up to 2 weeks.

TIP You can also make delicate, bite-sized chocolate crackles to serve with coffee. Use 72 confectionery cases instead of the mini muffin paper cases.

75 g (2¾ oz/2½ cups) puffed rice cereal
90 g (3¼ oz/1 cup) desiccated coconut
250 g (9 oz) dark chocolate (54 per cent cocoa solids), chopped
icing (confectioners') sugar, sifted, for dusting (optional)

makes
36

White chocolate and raspberry cheesecakes

125 g (4½ oz) plain sweet biscuits (cookies)

90 g (3¼ oz/⅓ cup) unsalted butter, melted

150 g (5½ oz) raspberries, to serve

Filling

125 g (4½ oz) white chocolate, chopped

125 ml (4 fl oz/½ cup) cream

200 g (7 oz) cream cheese

185 g (6½ oz/¾ cup) sour cream

55 g (2 oz/¼ cup) caster (superfine) sugar

3 eggs, at room temperature

300 g (10½ oz) frozen raspberries, thawed

makes
8

Preheat the oven to 150°C (300°F/Gas 2). Line eight holes of two six-hole giant muffin tins with paper muffin cases.

Place the biscuits in the bowl of a food processor and process until finely crushed. Add the melted butter and process until combined. Spoon into the prepared tins and press down firmly with the back of a spoon. Chill until required.

To make the filling, stir the chocolate and cream in a small saucepan over low heat until the chocolate has melted. Remove from the heat and allow to cool. Place the cream cheese in the cleaned bowl of the food processor and process until smooth. Add the sour cream, sugar, eggs and chocolate mixture and process until smooth. Gently stir in the raspberries.

Spoon the filling into the tins. Bake for 40 minutes, or until just set and the centres wobble slightly. Turn off the oven and leave the door slightly ajar, allowing the cheesecakes to cool for 1 hour. Transfer the tins to a wire rack to cool completely.

Chill the cheesecakes for 2 hours before serving. Remove from the tins and serve sprinkled with the raspberries.

These cheesecakes will keep, stored in an airtight container in the refrigerator, for up to 3 days.

Cherry and almond chocolate bark

200 g (7 oz) dark chocolate (70 per cent
   cocoa solids), chopped
55 g (2 oz/⅓ cup) dried cherries
40 g (1½ oz/¼ cup) slivered almonds,
   lightly toasted

makes
25

Line a baking tray with baking paper. Place the chocolate in a heatproof bowl over a saucepan of simmering water, ensuring the bowl doesn't touch the water. Stir until the chocolate has melted. Remove from the heat.

Pour the chocolate onto the tray and spread evenly into a 20 cm (8 inch) square. Tap the tray on the bench to settle the chocolate. Sprinkle on cherries and almonds. Stand in a cool place for 3–4 hours, or until the chocolate has set.

Break the chocolate bark into 4 cm (1½ inch) pieces.

This chocolate bark will keep, stored in an airtight container in a cool spot, for up to 2 weeks.

TIPS: Dried cherries are available from selected health food and gourmet food stores. You can replace the dried cherries with sweetened dried cranberries, if you wish.

Toast the almonds in a 180°C (350°F/Gas 4) oven for 5 minutes, or until lightly golden and aromatic. Allow to cool on the tray.

Chocolate orange fudge

395 g (13¾ oz) tin sweetened condensed milk

50 g (1¾ oz) unsalted butter, cubed

200 g (7 oz) orange-flavoured dark chocolate,
    finely chopped

200 g (7 oz) dark chocolate (54 per cent cocoa
    solids), finely chopped

makes
36

Line the base and sides of an 18 cm (7 inch) square cake tin with baking paper, extending the paper over two opposite sides for easy removal later.

Place the condensed milk and the butter in a heavy-based saucepan and cook over low heat, stirring occasionally, until the butter has melted. Bring just to a simmer, stirring frequently. Remove from the heat and set aside for 5 minutes to cool slightly. Add both types of the chocolate and stir until the chocolate has melted.

Working quickly, pour the fudge mixture into the prepared tin and use the back of a metal spoon to smooth the surface. Place in the refrigerator for 4 hours, or until firm.

Remove the fudge from the tin and cut into 3 cm (1¼ inch) squares.

This fudge will keep, with the layers separated by baking paper, stored in an airtight container in the refrigerator, for up to 1 month.

TIP Don't use orange-flavoured chocolate with a soft or liquid centre.

Triple chocolate fudge cookies

200 g (7 oz) dark chocolate, chopped

125 g (4½ oz) unsalted butter, softened

115 g (4 oz/½ cup) soft brown sugar

2 eggs, at room temperature

155 g (5½ oz/1¼ cups) plain (all-purpose) flour

40 g (1½ oz/⅓ cup) self-raising flour

125 g (4½ oz) good-quality milk chocolate,
roughly chopped

125 g (4½ oz) good-quality white chocolate,
roughly chopped

makes
35

Place the dark chocolate in a heatproof bowl over a saucepan of simmering water, ensuring the bowl doesn't touch the water. Stir until the chocolate has melted. Set aside, stirring occasionally, until cooled to room temperature.

Cream the butter and sugar in a large bowl using electric beaters until pale and fluffy. Add the eggs one at a time, beating well after each addition. Beat in the cooled, melted chocolate. Sift in the flours, add the milk chocolate and white chocolate and, using a wooden spoon, stir to combine. Cover with plastic wrap and refrigerate for 1 hour, or until firm enough to roll.

Preheat the oven to 180°C (350°F/Gas 4). Line two baking trays with baking paper.

Roll tablespoons of the mixture into balls, place on the prepared trays 5 cm (2 inches) apart and flatten slightly. Bake for 10 minutes, or until the cookies are still slightly soft to touch. Allow to cool on the trays for 5 minutes, cool completely on a wire rack. Repeat with the remaining mixture.

These cookies will keep, stored in an airtight container, for up to 1 week.

Double chocolate mud brownies

50 g (9 oz) dark chocolate (54 per cent cocoa
 solids), chopped
150 g (5½ oz) unsalted butter, cubed
170 g (6 oz/¾ cup) caster (superfine) sugar
3 eggs, at room temperature, lightly whisked
60 g (2¼ oz/½ cup) plain (all-purpose) flour
½ teaspoon baking powder
150 g (5½ oz) milk chocolate, roughly chopped
unsweetened cocoa powder or icing (confectioners')
 sugar, sifted, for dusting

makes
25

Preheat the oven to 160°C (315°F/Gas 2–3). Grease a 20 cm (8 inch) square cake tin and line the base and two opposite sides with baking paper, extending the paper over the sides for easy removal later.

Place the dark chocolate and butter in a heatproof bowl over a saucepan of simmering water, ensuring that the bowl doesn't touch the water. Stir until the chocolate and butter have melted. Remove from the heat and set aside to cool to lukewarm.

Add the sugar and eggs to the chocolate mixture and whisk until well combined. Sift in the flour and baking powder and whisk until just combined, then, using a wooden spoon, stir in the milk chocolate. Pour into the prepared tin and bake for 45–50 minutes, or until moist crumbs cling to a skewer inserted in the centre. Set aside to cool in the tin.

Remove the brownie from the tin, using the baking paper. Cut into 4 cm (1½ inch) squares. Dust with the cocoa or icing sugar and serve.

These brownies will keep, stored in an airtight container at room temperature, for up to 5 days.

White chocolate and macadamia biscotti

180 g (6¼ oz) unsalted butter, melted
and cooled
230 g (8¼ oz/1 cup) caster (superfine) sugar
3 eggs, at room temperature
finely grated zest of 3 lemons
1 teaspoon natural vanilla extract
200 g (7 oz) white chocolate, chopped
120 g (4¼ oz) macadamia nut halves
375 g (13 oz/3 cups) plain (all-purpose) flour
1 teaspoon baking powder

makes about
70

Preheat the oven to 160°C (315°F/Gas 2–3). Line two baking trays with baking paper.

Combine the melted butter, sugar, eggs, lemon zest and vanilla in a large bowl and whisk with a fork until well combined. Stir in the chocolate and macadamia nuts. In a separate bowl, sift together the flour and baking powder. Add to the butter mixture and stir with a wooden spoon to form a soft, slightly sticky dough. Divide the mixture into four equal portions. Transfer each portion to a lightly floured surface and shape into a 5 x 20 cm (2 x 8 inch) log. Place on the prepared trays 7 cm (2¾ inches) apart, allowing room for spreading, and flatten each log slightly with your hands. Bake, swapping the trays halfway through cooking, for 30–35 minutes, or until the logs are firm to touch and are just cooked through. Set aside to cool on the trays.

Reduce the oven to 150°C (300°F/Gas 2). Use a sharp knife to cut two logs diagonally into 1 cm (½ inch) thick slices. Spread the biscotti well apart on the trays. Bake, turning them over halfway through cooking, for 20 minutes, or until the biscotti are crisp and just starting to colour. Allow to cool on the trays. Repeat with the remaining logs.

These biscotti will keep, stored in an airtight container, for up to 2 weeks.

Chocolate meringues

2 egg whites, at room temperature
pinch of salt
115 g (4 oz/½ cup) caster (superfine) sugar
75 g (2¾ oz) dark chocolate (70 per cent cocoa solids), coarsely grated
unsweetened cocoa powder, sifted, for dusting (optional)

makes
24

Preheat the oven to 120°C (235°F/Gas ½). Line two baking trays with baking paper.

Beat the egg whites and salt in a medium bowl using electric beaters until soft peaks form. Add the sugar, a spoonful at a time, and beat until the sugar has dissolved, the mixture is thick and glossy and a long trailing peak forms when the beater is lifted. Use a large metal spoon to fold in the chocolate.

Spoon large teaspoonfuls of the mixture onto the prepared trays about 2 cm (¾ inch) apart. Dust with the cocoa, if desired.

Place the meringues in the oven and immediately reduce the temperature to 100°C (200°F/Gas ½). Bake for 1½ hours, or until the meringues are crisp and sound hollow when tapped on the base. Turn the oven off, leaving door slightly ajar and leave the meringues to cool slowly.

These meringues will keep, stored in an airtight container, for up to 1 week.

Chocolate peanut butter cups

300 g (10½ oz) dark chocolate (54 per cent cocoa
   solids), chopped
125 g (4½ oz/½ cup) smooth or crunchy peanut
   butter
30 g (1 oz /¼ cup) icing (confectioners') sugar
40 g (1½ oz/¼ cup) roasted unsalted peanuts,
   chopped

makes
20

Place 220 g (7¾ oz) of the chocolate in a heatproof
bowl over a saucepan of simmering water, ensuring
the base of the bowl doesn't touch the water. Stir
until the chocolate has melted. Remove from the
heat. Divide the chocolate among 20 small fluted
foil cases, using a teaspoon to spread the chocolate
evenly up the sides to form a thin layer. Set aside for
20 minutes, or until the chocolate has cooled slightly.

Meanwhile, place the remaining chocolate in a
heatproof bowl over a saucepan of simmering water,
ensuring the bowl doesn't touch the water. Stir until
the chocolate has melted. Remove from the heat. Stir
in the peanut butter and sugar. Spoon the filling into
a piping (icing) bag fitted with a 1 cm (½ inch) plain
nozzle. Pipe the filling into the chocolate cups. Top
each cup with the chopped peanuts and set aside in a
cool place for 1 hour, or until the filling firms slightly.

These chocolate cups will keep, stored in an airtight
container, for up to 1 week.

Chocolate caramel tartlets

Tart cases

110 g (3¾ oz) plain (all-purpose) flour

½ teaspoon baking powder

90 g (3¼ oz/1 cup) desiccated coconut

95 g (3¼ oz/½ cup) soft brown sugar

125 g (4½ oz/½ cup) unsalted butter, melted

1 teaspoon natural vanilla extract

Caramel filling

395 g (14 oz) tin sweetened condensed milk

95 g (3½ oz/½ cup) soft brown sugar

80 g (2¾ oz) unsalted butter, cubed

2 tablespoons golden syrup (light treacle)

Chocolate topping

200 g (7 oz) dark chocolate, chopped

30 g (1 oz) unsalted butter, cubed

makes
42

Preheat the oven to 180°C (350°F/Gas 4). Grease 42 holes of four 12-hole mini muffin tins.

To make the tart cases, sift the flour and baking powder into a bowl, add the coconut and sugar and stir with a wooden spoon. Stir in the butter and vanilla until combined. Divide the mixture among the tins, pressing firmly into the bases and sides. Bake for 12 minutes, or until light golden and crisp.

To make the filling, stir the condensed milk, sugar, butter and golden syrup in a heavy-based saucepan over low heat until the sugar has dissolved. Bring to a simmer and cook, stirring constantly, for 5 minutes, or until the mixture darkens slightly.

Immediately spoon the filling into the tartlet cases. Bake for 5–8 minutes, until the caramel is bubbling around the edges. Cool in the tins for 10 minutes, then use a small spatula to transfer the tartlets to a wire rack to cool completely.

To make the topping, combine the chocolate and butter in a heatproof bowl over a saucepan of simmering water, ensuring the bowl doesn't touch the water. Stir until the chocolate and butter have melted. Remove from the heat. Spread a thick layer of chocolate over the top of the tartlets. Stand in a cool place for 4–6 hours, or until the chocolate has set.

Chocolate caramel tartlets will keep, stored in an airtight container, for up to 2 weeks.

Hazelnut meringues with chocolate ganache

Preheat the oven to 100°C (200°F/Gas ½). Draw two 12 x 20 cm (4½ x 8 inch) rectangles each on three pieces of baking paper and place on three baking trays, with the pencil marks facing down.

Place the hazelnuts in the bowl of a food processor and process until finely ground.

Beat the egg whites and a pinch salt in a large bowl using electric beaters until soft peaks form. Add the sugar, a spoonful at a time, and beat until very thick and glossy and all the sugar has dissolved. Use a large metal spoon or spatula to fold the hazelnuts into the meringue mixture. Divide the meringue evenly among the marked rectangles on the prepared trays and use the back of a spoon to spread out evenly. Bake, rotating the trays every 20 minutes, for 1 hour, or until crisp. Turn off the oven and leave the meringue rectangles in the oven for 2 hours, or until cooled to room temperature.

100 g (3½ oz) hazelnuts, toasted and skinned

4 egg whites, at room temperature

230 g (8 oz/1 cup) caster (superfine) sugar

60 g (2¼ oz) dark chocolate (54 per cent cocoa solids), chopped

10 g (¼ oz) unsalted butter, cubed

Chocolate ganache

150 g (5½ oz) dark chocolate (54 per cent cocoa solids), chopped

125 ml (4 fl oz/½ cup) cream

1½ tablespoons Frangelico

makes
12

Meanwhile, to make the ganache, combine the chocolate and cream in a small saucepan over low heat and stir until the chocolate has melted. Stir in the Frangelico, and then set aside to cool to a thin, spreadable consistency.

Spread half the chocolate ganache over two of the meringue rectangles. Top each with another meringue rectangle, spread on the remaining ganache and finish with a layer of meringue, to form two meringue stacks. Cover with plastic wrap and refrigerate for 30 minutes, or until the ganache is firm.

Place the chocolate and butter in a heatproof bowl over a saucepan of simmering water, ensuring the bowl doesn't touch the water. Stir until the chocolate has melted.

Carefully transfer the meringue stacks to a cutting board. Use a sharp knife to cut each stack into six slices. Drizzle with the chocolate mixture and stand at room temperature for at least 30 minutes.

Hazelnut meringues with chocolate ganache will keep, stored in an airtight container at room temperature, for up to 2 days.

Chocolate, blackberry and coconut slice

180 g (6¼ oz/2 cups) desiccated coconut

250 g (9 oz/2 cups) plain (all-purpose) flour, sifted

165 g (5¾ oz/¾ cup) soft brown sugar

200 g (7 oz) dark chocolate (54 per cent cocoa solids), chopped

100 g (3½ oz) unsalted butter, chopped

2 eggs, at room temperature, lightly whisked

160 g (5¾ oz/½ cup) blackberry jam

icing (confectioners') sugar, sifted, for dusting

makes
28

Preheat the oven to 170°C (325°F/Gas 3). Line the base and sides of an 18 x 28 cm (7 x 11¼ inch) baking tin with baking paper, extending the paper over two long sides for easy removal later.

Combine the coconut, flour and brown sugar in a large bowl and set aside.

Place the chocolate and butter in a small saucepan and stir over low heat until the chocolate and butter have melted. Add to the coconut mixture with the eggs and stir with a wooden spoon until combined.

Spoon half the chocolate mixture into the prepared tin and press down firmly with the back of a spoon. Spread the jam over the top, then add the remaining chocolate mixture, pressing with the back of the spoon to smooth the surface.

Bake for 50 minutes, or until a skewer inserted in the centre of the slice comes out clean. Allow to cool in the tin for 10 minutes, then transfer to a wire rack to cool completely. Cut into 4 x 4.5 cm (1½ x 1¾ inch) pieces and serve dusted with the icing sugar.

This slice will keep, stored in an airtight container, for up to 5 days.

Milk chocolate and cashew truffles

150 g (5½ oz) milk chocolate, chopped

60 ml (2 fl oz/¼ cup) cream

1 tablespoon Kahlua or Tia Maria

60 g (2¼ oz) unsalted cashew nuts, lightly
toasted and finely chopped

makes
18

Place the chocolate and cream in a heatproof bowl over a saucepan of simmering water, ensuring the base of the bowl doesn't touch the water. Stir until the chocolate has melted. Remove from the heat and stir in the liqueur. Cover with plastic wrap and transfer to the refrigerator for 1–2 hours, stirring occasionally, or until the mixture is firm enough to roll into balls.

Spread the cashew nuts on a plate. Roll teaspoons of the chocolate mixture into balls, then roll in the cashew nuts to coat. Place the finished truffles in paper cases, if desired, transfer to a plate and return to the refrigerator for at least 1 hour before serving.

These truffles will keep, stored in an airtight container in the refrigerator, for up to 2 weeks.

TIP Toast the cashews in a preheated 180°C (350°F/ Gas 4) oven for 8–10 minutes, or until golden and aromatic. Cool on the tray, then chop.

White chocolate and lime truffles

80 ml (2½ fl oz/⅓ cup) thick (double/heavy) cream
600 g (1 lb 5 oz) white chocolate, chopped
3 teaspoons finely grated lime zest
lime zest strips, to decorate

makes
36

Place the cream and half the chocolate in a heatproof bowl over a saucepan of simmering water, ensuring the base of the bowl doesn't touch the water. Stir until the chocolate has melted. Remove from the heat, add the grated zest, cover and then chill for 30 minutes.

Grease a 17 cm (6½ inch) square cake tin and line the base and sides with baking paper. Line a baking tray with baking paper.

Beat the chocolate mixture using electric beaters for 3 minutes. Spoon into the prepared tin and smooth the surface with the back of a spoon. Chill for 2 hours, or until firm.

Turn out the chocolate mixture onto a cutting board. Trim the edges, then cut into 2.5 cm (1 inch) squares. Transfer the squares to the prepared tray. Freeze for 20 minutes.

Meanwhile, place the remaining chocolate in a heatproof bowl over a saucepan of simmering water, ensuring the bowl doesn't touch the water. Stir until the chocolate has melted. Remove from the heat.

Using two forks, dip the chocolate squares, one at a time, into the melted chocolate, allowing any excess to drip off. Return to the tray, immediately place a strip of lime zest on each square and stand in a cool place until the chocolate has set.

These truffles will keep, stored in a single layer in an airtight container in a cool place, for up to 2 days.

Chocolate and pecan honey wafers

35 g (1¼ oz) plain (all-purpose) flour

25 g (1 oz) caster (superfine) sugar

85 g (3 oz) honey (such as iron bark or blue gum), warmed slightly

65 g (2½ oz) unsalted butter, melted and cooled

1 egg white

70 g (2½ oz) dark chocolate, roughly chopped

70 g (2½ oz) pecans, roughly chopped

makes
25

Preheat the oven to 160°C (315°F/Gas 2–3). Line two baking trays with baking paper.

Combine the flour, sugar, honey, butter and egg white in the bowl of a food processor and process until just combined. Divide the mixture between the baking trays and spread with the back of a spoon to form two thin 20 x 25 cm (8 x 10 inch) rectangles of equal thickness. Sprinkle evenly with chocolate and pecans.

Bake, swapping the trays halfway through cooking, for 24–28 minutes, or until dark golden. Allow to cool on the trays.

Break into pieces roughly 5 cm (2 inches) and serve.

These wafers will keep, stored in an airtight container, for up to 1 week.

Striped chocolate fingers

100 g (3½ oz) unsalted butter, softened

75 g (2¾ oz/⅓ cup) sugar

1 teaspoon natural vanilla extract

1 egg, at room temperature

125 g (4½ oz/1 cup) plain (all-purpose) flour

½ teaspoon baking powder

1 tablespoon unsweetened cocoa powder, sifted

1 tablespoon plain (all-purpose) flour, extra, sifted

makes
70

Cream the butter, sugar and vanilla in a bowl using electric beaters until pale and fluffy. Add the egg and beat until just combined. Sift in the flour and baking powder and stir until a soft dough forms.

Divide the dough in half and transfer to a lightly floured surface. Gently knead the cocoa into one portion and the extra flour into the other portion. Divide each portion of dough in half, cover with plastic wrap and refrigerate until firm.

Line a baking tray with baking paper. Roll out each portion of dough on a lightly floured work surface to form a 7.5 x 25 cm (3 x 10 inch) rectangle. Place a chocolate rectangle on the prepared tray, top with a plain rectangle and press down lightly. Repeat with the remaining rectangle layers, finishing with a plain layer. Cover with plastic wrap and chill for 2 hours.

Preheat the oven to 160°C (315°F/Gas 2–3). Line two baking trays with baking paper.

Transfer the dough block to a cutting board. Trim the edges, then cut into 3 mm (⅛ inch) thick slices. Place the slices about 1.5 cm (⅝ inch) apart on the prepared trays. Bake, swapping the trays halfway through cooking, for 15 minutes, or until the biscuits just start to colour. Allow to cool on the trays.

These fingers will keep, stored in an airtight container, for up to 2 weeks.

Chocolate oranges

2 medium valencia oranges, ends trimmed, cut into
   5 mm (¼ inch) thick slices
100 g (3½ oz) dark chocolate (54 per cent cocoa
   solids), chopped

makes
40

Preheat the oven to 120°C (235°F/Gas ½). Line a wire rack with baking paper and place over a baking tray.

Spread the orange slices on the prepared rack and bake, turning halfway through cooking, for 2½ hours, or until dried but not coloured. Turn off the oven and allow the oranges to cool in the oven.

Place the chocolate in a small heatproof bowl over a saucepan of simmering water, ensuring the bowl doesn't touch the water. Stir until the chocolate has melted. Remove from the heat.

Line a tray with baking paper. Dip half of each orange slice into the chocolate, tapping gently on the side of the bowl to remove any excess. Place on the prepared tray and stand in a cool place until the chocolate has set.

The dried orange slices (without the chocolate) will keep, stored in an airtight container, for up to 1 week. Once dipped in the chocolate they will keep for 1 day.

TIP The time that the chocolate takes to set depends on the weather: the cooler the weather, the less time it takes.

Melt-and-mix chocolate cakes

150 g (5½ oz) unsalted butter, cubed

230 g (8 oz/1 cup) soft brown sugar

185 ml (6 fl oz/¾ cup) freshly made espresso
   coffee

2 eggs, at room temperature, lightly whisked

125 g (4½ oz/1 cup) self-raising flour

30 g (1 oz/¼ cup) plain (all-purpose) flour

60 g (2¼ oz/½ cup) unsweetened cocoa powder

¼ teaspoon bicarbonate of soda (baking soda)

icing (confectioners') sugar, sifted, for dusting

Chocolate butter cream

250 g (9 oz/2 cups) icing (confectioners')
   sugar, sifted

2 tablespoons unsweetened cocoa powder

60 g (2¼ oz/¼ cup) unsalted butter, softened

2 tablespoons hot water

makes
12

Preheat the oven to 180°C (350°F/Gas 4). Line a 12-hole standard muffin tin with paper cases.

Combine the butter, brown sugar and coffee in a saucepan over medium heat. Stir until the butter has melted and the sugar has dissolved. Remove from the heat and cool slightly.

Whisk the eggs into the butter mixture. In a separate bowl, sift together the flours, cocoa and bicarbonate of soda. Stir half the flour mixture into the butter mixture until just combined. Add the remaining flour mixture and stir until just combined. Transfer the mixture to a jug and pour into the prepared tin. Bake for 20 minutes, or until a skewer inserted in the centre of a cake comes out clean. Allow the cakes to cool in the tin for 3 minutes, then transfer to a wire rack to cool completely.

To make the butter cream, place 125 g (4½ oz/1 cup) of the sugar in a large bowl, add the cocoa, butter and water and beat with electric beaters until smooth and creamy. Gradually add the remaining sugar and beat until the butter cream is thick.

Spread the butter cream over the cooled cakes using a spatula or flat-bladed knife.

The un-iced cakes will keep, stored in an airtight container, for up to 5 days. Iced cakes will keep in the same way for up to 2 days.

Turkish delight and pistachio rocky road bites

400 g (14 oz) dark chocolate (54 per cent cocoa solids), chopped

110 g (3¾ oz) Turkish delight, cubed

60 g (2¼ oz/1 cup) shredded coconut

100 g (3½ oz/¾ cup) pistachio nuts, lightly toasted and coarsely chopped

icing (confectioners') sugar, sifted, for dusting (optional)

makes
36

Line the base and long sides of a 16 x 26 cm (6¼ x 10½ inch) baking tin with baking paper, allowing the paper to overhang the sides.

Place the chocolate in a heatproof bowl over a saucepan of simmering water, ensuring the base of the bowl doesn't touch the water. Stir until the chocolate has melted. Remove from the heat and set aside, stirring occasionally, to cool to room temperature.

Add the Turkish delight, coconut and pistachio nuts to the cooled chocolate and stir to combine. Spoon into the tin and use the back of the spoon to spread. Lightly tap the tin on the bench to settle the mixture. Stand in a cool place for 1–4 hours, or until the chocolate has set (this will depend on the weather).

Transfer the rocky road to a cutting board and use a 3 cm (1¼ inch) cookie cutter dipped in cornflour to cut into rounds. Dust with the sugar, if desired, and place in small paper cases to serve.

These rocky road bites will keep, stored in an airtight container in a cool place, for up to 1 month.

Chocolate, date and walnut tortes

Preheat the oven to 160°C (315°F/Gas 2–3). Brush eight 8 cm (3¼ inch) loose-based fluted flan (tart) tins with the oil and line the bases with rounds of baking paper. Place the tins on a baking tray.

Beat the egg whites in a large bowl using electric beaters until soft peaks form. Beat in the sugar, a tablespoon at a time, until thick and glossy.

Use a large metal spoon to fold the chocolate, walnuts, dates and cocoa into the meringue mixture. Divide the mixture among the prepared tins and smooth the surfaces with the back of a spoon. Bake for 40 minutes, or until the tortes start to pull away slightly from the edge of the tins. Turn off the oven and allow the tortes to cool in the oven with the door slightly ajar.

Remove the tortes from the tins and transfer to serving plates. Serve accompanied by the cream.

These tortes will keep, stored in an airtight container, for up to 2 days.

vegetable oil, to grease

4 egg whites, at room temperature

80 g (2¾ oz/⅓ cup) caster (superfine) sugar

150 g (5½ oz) dark chocolate (54 per cent cocoa solids), chopped

150 g (5½ oz/1½ cups) walnut halves, chopped

120 g (4¼ oz/⅔ cup) pitted dates, chopped

1 tablespoon unsweetened cocoa powder, sifted

cream, lightly whipped, to serve

makes
8

Chocolate mud cookies

250 g (9 oz/1²/₃ cups) chopped dark chocolate

125 g (4½ oz/½ cup) unsalted butter, softened

185 g (6½ oz/1 cup) soft brown sugar

1 teaspoon natural vanilla extract

1 egg

185 g (6½ oz/1½ cups) plain (all-purpose) flour

40 g (1½ oz/⅓ cup) unsweetened cocoa powder

makes
36

Preheat the oven to 180°C (350°F/Gas 4). Line two baking trays with baking paper.

Place the chocolate in a food processor and pulse until finely chopped, then set aside.

Cream the butter, sugar and vanilla in a medium bowl using electric beaters until pale and fluffy, then add the egg, beating until just combined. Sift in the flour and cocoa, add the chopped chocolate and stir with a wooden spoon to form a soft dough.

Shape tablespoons of the dough into balls, place on the prepared trays well apart and flatten into 4.5 cm (1¾ inch) rounds. Bake for 9 minutes. Allow to cool on the trays for a few minutes, then transfer to a wire rack to cool completely.

These cookies will keep, stored in an airtight container, for up to 1 week.

Walnut and fig hedgehog bars

100 g (3½ oz) digestive or shredded wheatmeal
    biscuits (cookies), broken into
    2 cm (¾ inch) pieces
125 g (4½ oz/⅔ cup) chopped dried figs
50 g (1¾ oz/½ cup) walnut halves, roughly
    chopped
300 g (10½ oz) dark chocolate (54 per cent cocoa
    solids), chopped
60 g (2¼ oz/¼ cup) unsalted butter, chopped
90 g (3¼ oz/¼ cup) honey
icing (confectioners') sugar or sweetened cocoa
    powder, sifted, for dusting (optional)

makes
21

Line the base and sides of an 18 cm (7 inch) square cake tin with baking paper, extending the paper over two opposite sides for easy removal later.

Combine the biscuits, figs and walnuts in a medium bowl and set aside.

Place the chocolate, butter and honey in a small saucepan and stir over low heat until the chocolate and butter have melted. Add to the biscuit mixture and stir with a wooden spoon to combine. Spoon into the prepared tin and tap gently on the bench to settle the mixture. Cover with plastic wrap and refrigerate for 1 hour, or until firm. Remove from the tin and cut into 2.5 x 6 cm (1 x 2½ inch) bars. To serve, dust with the sugar or cocoa, if desired.

These bars will keep, stored in an airtight container in the refrigerator, for up to 1

Decadent double choc mousse cupcakes

90 g (3¼ oz/¾ cup) plain (all-purpose) flour

30 g (1 oz/¼ cup) self-raising flour

125 g (4½ oz) unsalted butter, chopped

230 g (8½ oz/1 cup) caster (superfine) sugar

100 g (3½ oz) white chocolate, chopped

1 egg

1 teaspoon natural vanilla extract

125 ml (4 fl oz/½ cup) milk

Chocolate mousse

1 egg yolk

2 tablespoons caster (superfine) sugar

500 ml (17 fl oz/2 cups) cream, for whipping

375 g (13 oz) dark chocolate chips, melted

makes
24

Preheat the oven to 160°C (315°F/Gas 2–3). Line 24 standard muffin holes with paper cases.

Sift the flours together in a bowl and make a well. Place the butter, sugar and chocolate in a saucepan and stir over low heat until the sugar has dissolved. Remove from the heat and cool slightly.

Whisk the egg, vanilla and milk until combined, then pour into the well in the flour, together with the chocolate mixture, and whisk to combine. Divide the mixture among the cases, until half-full. Bake for 15 minutes, or until a skewer comes out clean when inserted into the centre. Leave to cool completely on a wire rack.

To make the chocolate mousse, place the egg yolk and sugar in a small bowl and whisk over a small saucepan of simmering water until thick and creamy.

Beat the cream in a bowl with electric beaters until soft peaks form. Add the melted chocolate and the egg mixture and continue to beat for 1–2 minutes, or until thickened. Decorate the cakes with the mousse, then place them on a tray and refrigerate for 1 hour, or until set. Sprinkle with cocoa before serving.

Milk chocolate buttons

75 g (2½ oz) unsalted butter
75 g (2½ oz) milk chocolate, chopped
80 g (2¾ oz/⅓ cup) soft brown sugar
2 eggs, lightly beaten
60 g (2¼ oz/½ cup) self-raising flour, sifted

Ganache
80 g (2¾ oz) milk chocolate, chopped
2 tablespoons thick (double/heavy) cream
silver cachous, to decorate

makes
12

Preheat the oven to 160°C (315°F/Gas 2–3) and line 12 mini muffin holes with paper cases.

Place the butter and chocolate in a heatproof bowl and sit the bowl over a saucepan of simmering water, making sure the bowl doesn't touch the water. Stir the chocolate until melted. Remove from the heat and mix in the sugar and egg. Stir in the flour.

Transfer the mixture to a jug and pour evenly among the cases. Bake for 20–25 minutes, or until cooked. Leave in the tin for 10 minutes, then transfer on to a wire rack to cool completely.

To make the ganache, place the chocolate and cream in a heatproof bowl. Sit the bowl over a saucepan of simmering water, making sure the bowl doesn't touch the water. Once the chocolate has almost melted, remove the bowl from the heat and stir until the remaining chocolate has melted and the mixture is smooth. Allow to cool for about 8 minutes, or until thickened slightly.

Return the cakes to the cold tin to keep them stable while you spread 1 heaped teaspoon of ganache over each cake. Decorate with silver cachous.

Chocolate pecan and golden syrup tarts

unsweetened cocoa powder or icing (confectioners')
sugar, sifted, for dusting

Chocolate pastry

185 g (6½ oz/1½ cups) plain (all-purpose) flour,
sifted

2 tablespoons unsweetened cocoa powder, sifted

2 tablespoons icing (confectioners') sugar, sifted

150 g (5½ oz) unsalted butter, chilled and cubed

2 tablespoons chilled water

Filling

75 g (2¾ oz) dark chocolate (54 per cent cocoa
solids), chopped

75 g (2¾ oz) unsalted butter, cubed

1 egg, at room temperature

1 egg yolk, at room temperature

2 tablespoons golden syrup (light treacle)

1½ tablespoons caster (superfine) sugar

50 g (1¾ oz/½ cup) pecans, lightly toasted
and chopped

makes
6

To make the pastry, combine the flour, cocoa, sugar and butter in the bowl of a food processor and process until the mixture resembles fine breadcrumbs. Add the water and pulse until just combined. Turn out onto a lightly floured work surface and knead for 1–2 minutes, or until the dough just comes together. Divide the dough in half and shape each portion into a disc. Cover with plastic wrap and refrigerate for 15 minutes.

Roll out one portion of dough to 3 mm (⅛ inch) thick. Cut out three 12 cm (4½ inch) rounds, re-rolling if necessary. Line three 8 cm (3¼ inch) loose-based fluted flan (tart) tins and trim the edges. Repeat with the remaining dough. Transfer the tins to a baking tray and freeze for 40 minutes.

Preheat the oven to 200°C (400°F/Gas 6). Bake the pastry cases for 15 minutes, or until they are just cooked and dry.

Meanwhile, to make the filling, place the chocolate and butter in a small saucepan over low heat and stir until melted. Remove from the heat. Combine the egg, egg yolk, golden syrup and sugar in a bowl and whisk well. Stir in the chocolate mixture and transfer to a jug.

Reduce the oven to 180°C (350°F/Gas 4). Pour the chocolate mixture into the warm pastry cases, then sprinkle on the pecans. Bake for 15 minutes, or until the filling is puffed. Serve warm, dusted with the cocoa or sugar.

These tarts will keep, stored in an airtight container, for up to 4 days. (For image, see page 248.)

Chocolate hazelnut wheels

100 g (3½ oz) unsalted butter, softened

55 g (2 oz/¼ cup) caster (superfine) sugar

1 egg, at room temperature

125 g (4½ oz/1 cup) plain (all-purpose) flour

30 g (1 oz/¼ cup) unsweetened cocoa powder

55 g (2 oz/½ cup) ground hazelnuts

70 g (2½ oz/½ cup) hazelnuts, toasted, skinned
  and chopped

Chocolate filling

100 g (3½ oz) dark chocolate (54 per cent cocoa
  solids), chopped

50 g (1¾ oz) butter, softened

40 g (1½ oz/⅓ cup) icing (confectioners') sugar,
  sifted

makes
16

Beat the butter and sugar in a large bowl using electric beaters until just combined, then add the egg, beating until just combined. Sift in the flour and cocoa, add the ground hazelnuts and, using a wooden spoon, stir to form a soft dough. Shape into a flat disc, cover with plastic wrap and refrigerate for 30 minutes.

Preheat the oven to 180°C (350°F/Gas 4). Line two baking trays with baking paper.

Roll out the dough on a lightly floured work surface until 5 mm (¼ inch) thick. Chill for 30 minutes, then cut the dough into 32 rounds using a 5 cm (2 inch) cookie cutter, re-rolling the dough when necessary. Place on the prepared trays, then refrigerate for 10 minutes.

Bake, swapping the trays halfway through cooking, for 15 minutes, or until the biscuits are cooked through and aromatic. Allow to cool completely on the trays.

Meanwhile, to make the chocolate filling, place the chocolate in a heatproof bowl over a saucepan of simmering water, ensuring the bowl doesn't touch the water. Stir until the chocolate has melted. Set aside to cool to room temperature. Beat the cooled, melted chocolate with the butter using electric beaters until creamy. Add the sugar and beat until well combined.

Use the chocolate filling to sandwich the biscuits together, spreading the filling around the sides of the sandwiched biscuits. Roll the sides of the biecuits in the chopped hazelnuts.

The filled biscuits will keep, stored in an airtight container, for up to 5 days. Unfilled biscuits will keep, stored in an airtight container, for up to 2 weeks. (For image, see page 249.)

Index

Published in 2011 by Murdoch Books Pty Limited

Murdoch Books Australia
Pier 8/9, 23 Hickson Road
Millers Point NSW 2000
Phone: +61 (0) 2 8220 2000
Fax: +61 (0) 2 8220 2558
www.murdochbooks.com.au

Murdoch Books UK Limited
Erico House, 6th Floor
93–99 Upper Richmond Road
Putney, London SW15 2TG
Phone: +44 (0) 20 8785 5995
Fax: +44 (0) 20 8785 5985
www.murdochbooks.co.uk

Chief Executive: Juliet Rogers
Publishing Director: Chris Rennie

Publisher: Lynn Lewis
Cover Designer: Heather Menzies
Designers: Clare O'Loughlin, Heather Menzies.
Editor: Justine Harding
Editorial Coordinator: Liz Malcolm
Production: Alexandra Gonzalez
Index: Jo Rudd

National Library of Australia Cataloguing-in-Publication Data:
High tea: recipes with a sense of occasion.
ISBN: 978-1-74266-014-1 (pbk.)
Includes index.
Afternoon teas. Baking. Cake.
641.53

Printed by 1010 Printing International Limited, China